MASTERING
THE ART OF
PUBLIC
SPEAKING

D0068387

Also by Michael J. Gelb

The Art of Connection

Body Learning

Brain Power (with Kelly Howell)

Creativity on Demand

Da Vinci Decoded

Discover Your Genius

Five Keys to High Performance

The Healing Organization (with Raj Sisodia)

How to Think like Leonardo da Vinci

The How to Think like Leonardo da Vinci Workbook

Innovate like Edison (with Sarah Miller Caldicott)

Lessons from the Art of Juggling (with Tony Buzan)

Present Yourself!

Samurai Chess (with Grandmaster Raymond Keene)

Thinking for a Change

Wine Drinking for Inspired Thinking

MASTERING
THE ART OF
PUBLIC
SPEAKING

8 Secrets to Transform Fear and Supercharge Your Career

MICHAEL J. GELB

New World Library
Novato, California

New World Library
14 Pamaron Way
Novato, California 94949

Some of the ideas, examples, methods, and exercises in this book appeared in different forms in *Present Yourself!* and in other works by the author. They are reframed and contextualized here to be most useful and relevant to our present circumstances.

Text design by Tona Pearce Myers
Illustrations by Brian Weller (brianjweller.com)

Library of Congress Cataloging-in-Publication Data

Names: Gelb, Michael J., author.
Title: Mastering the art of public speaking : 8 secrets to transform fear and super-charge your career / Michael J. Gelb.
Description: Novato, California : New World Library, [2020] | Includes bibliographical references and index. | Summary: "An experienced presenter and executive coach shows readers how to speak effectively in a variety of situations, ranging from job interviews to wedding toasts. Topics include building rapport with audiences, managing performance anxiety, displaying appropriate body language, and using "mind maps" to organize and remember presentations."-- Provided by publisher.
Identifiers: LCCN 2020020607 (print) | LCCN 2020020608 (ebook) | ISBN 9781608686278 (paperback) | ISBN 9781608686285 (epub)
Subjects: LCSH: Public speaking | Business presentations.
Classification: LCC PN4192.B87 G46 2020 (print) | LCC PN4192.B87 (ebook) | DDC 808.5/1--dc23
LC record available at https://lccn.loc.gov/2020020607
LC ebook record available at https://lccn.loc.gov/2020020608

First printing, September 2020
ISBN 978-1-60868-627-8
Ebook ISBN 978-1-60868-628-5
Printed in Canada on 100% postconsumer-waste recycled paper

 New World Library is proud to be a Gold Certified Environmentally Responsible Publisher. Publisher certification awarded by Green Press Initiative.

10   9   8   7   6   5   4   3   2   1

This book is dedicated to the originator of
Mind Mapping and master of public speaking,
Tony Buzan (1942–2019).

Contents

Preface

Connect before Speaking

I'm a professional speaker. For more than forty years, people have been paying me to give presentations on creativity, innovation, and leadership. During this time, I've learned, and I continue to learn, a lot about what works and what doesn't work in presenting to all kinds of audiences. I'm also a professional executive coach, and over the years I've helped many clients overcome fear and develop confidence and poise so that they can deliver engaging, meaningful, and memorable messages, sometimes with high stakes involved.

I *love* helping people in this way! There's something especially wonderful when a client who is terrified of public speaking transforms that fear into confidence and then as a direct result becomes more successful in her career. The "Transform Fear and Supercharge Your Career" part of this book's subtitle comes from watching what happens when people apply the secrets you will learn in this book.

I've coached clients to prepare presentations in their quest to secure multimillion-dollar contracts and to inspire thousands of employees to align with a higher purpose in the face of challenging circumstances. I have coached many aspirants who are now successful professional speakers.

For many of my clients the ability to rise to the challenge of speaking effectively to larger and larger groups became the secret of their success and in many cases the turning point in their careers. And now many of my clients need help learning how to connect with and influence audiences via various online modalities. The principles and methods that will make you effective with an in-person audience become even more important when you are presenting online.

All my books are a response to one simple question: What skills, competencies, or insights do people need that I know the most about?

A few years ago my answer to that question was *relationship building*. So in 2017 New World Library released *The Art of Connection: 7 Relationship-Building Skills Every Leader Needs Now*. The book provides compelling evidence that our ability to connect effectively with others is the secret to leadership — and to health, happiness, and longevity.

This book builds on the fundamental skills covered in *The Art of Connection*. The core principle of connection is expressed in the motto *Conjungere ad solvedum*: Connect before solving. In other words, when you create rapport, alignment, and a sense of shared humanity with others, it becomes much easier to be creative and find innovative solutions to problems.

The same principle holds in public speaking. Our motto for this book is:

Conjungere ad orationem: Connect before speaking.

When you *connect* with yourself by organizing your nervous system — one of the most important secrets you will learn — and clarifying your message and objectives for your audience, you can then connect with others and establish the rapport that transforms fear into enthusiasm.

If you have read *The Art of Connection*, you'll discover that it has prepared you to get the most from this book. If you haven't, don't worry; it isn't a prerequisite to reading this book, but you may find that it's a perfect follow-up.

A Note about the Illustrations

In this book you will learn how to make Mind Maps to help you generate and organize your presentations. I use Mind Mapping to prepare all my presentations and to write all my books, including this one. You'll discover that when you are making your own Mind Maps, it's best to place just one key word on each line, and to follow the other guidelines for classic Mind Mapping, as described in chapter 3. The maplike images for each chapter, generated by our illustrious illustrator, Brian Weller, are designed to create an easily accessible and memorable summary/study guide for the book. These summary illustrations reference many of the important quotes and key phrases in each chapter to help you remember and apply the key information you need to master the art of public speaking.

Introduction

The #1 Fear Is the #1 Skill

Warren Buffett, the legendary Oracle of Omaha, was recently asked about the best investment any of us can make. He didn't suggest buying shares of Berkshire Hathaway or putting cash into real estate. Rather, he advised, "Invest in yourself."

How do we do that? Buffett explains, "The one easy way to become worth 50 percent more than you are now — at least — is to hone your communication skills — both written and verbal." He adds, "You can have all the brainpower in the world, but you have to be able to transmit it. And the transmission is communication."

Along with writing well, public speaking is the most powerful means of transmission. It is the #1 skill you can cultivate to supercharge your career. The ability to express yourself effectively, to one or to one thousand, is a critical key to success in sales, leadership, and life.

The basic elements of effective presentation are also essential to personal happiness.

Do you know how to ask for what you want? Can you formulate requests that others can readily fulfill? One of the simplest keys to happiness is knowing our most vital needs and enrolling others in helping us to fulfill those needs. We do this by developing our skill in advocating for what we want.

These same skills are essential if we want to be effective in changing the world for the better. If you want to help save the Earth, raise funds for a charity, or champion the rights of others, you'll need to speak in a compelling and memorable way.

In this book you will learn a simple, powerful, practical approach to improving your effectiveness in any kind of public-speaking situation, from a job interview to a formal speech, from a wedding toast to a eulogy. You'll learn to do this in a way that feels natural, enlivening, and enjoyable for both you and your audiences. You'll learn how to persuade, sell, engage, influence, inspire, and enroll others so you can become a powerful advocate for your ideas and ideals, both personally and professionally.

Learning to write well is, as Buffett suggests, also important, but it does not engender in us the same fear and resistance as public speaking. It's more difficult to learn to be a good writer than it is to be a good speaker, and as you rise in an organization, you have the luxury of delegating what is written in your name, but you can't do that with public speaking.

The Peter Principle:
The Cream Rises Until It Sours

In 1969, way before *Dilbert* and *The Office*, "hierarchiologist" Laurence J. Peter introduced the idea that in a hierarchy, every person tends to rise to his level of incompetence. His classic book, *The Peter Principle*, offers a satirical but wickedly accurate look at why things go awry in bureaucratic organizations. Peter writes,

"Bureaucracy defends the status quo long past the time when the quo has lost its status."

Whether you work in an organization or operate independently, you'll discover that many people find their level of incompetence through an inability to present effectively and to persuade or inspire others. Some people are competent in their one-to-one communication but can't speak effectively to small groups. Others are comfortable with groups of five or six but freeze up at the prospect of speaking to an audience of fifty or sixty. And some folks are okay with fifty or sixty people but panic at the thought of presenting to five or six thousand.

Your presentation skills become more important as you become more important. And to become more important, you need excellent presentation skills.

You must be able to sell your ideas to have them implemented. And communicating your ideas effectively helps you develop and refine your ideas.

The process of preparing a simple, powerful expression of complex ideas compels you to clarify your thoughts. You do not know what you are talking about unless you are able to articulate your message so that others can understand it.

Mastering the art of public speaking is a key to leadership and long-term success.

Many well-educated, hardworking people have seen their careers stalled because they haven't developed this art, while others have risen to the top of their fields by cultivating this essential leadership ability.

A financial analyst was promoted to director of research of a multibillion-dollar pension fund, largely as a result of a series of presentations he gave on the status of various industries. His boss had asked the research group to put together eight presentations, and he volunteered for the first one. When no one came forward to do the second one, he volunteered again. Same for all the rest. Shortly afterward, he was promoted. Then he was promoted to director of equity investments, and a few years later he was elevated to a vice presidency and directorship of the entire fund. He attributes much of his success to his commitment to mastering the art of public speaking:

> My devotion to continuous improvement of my communication and public speaking skills is the principal differentiating factor between myself and my competition in my career on three levels: first, by basing all my presentations on careful listening and sensitivity to my clients' needs I build their confidence and gain their trust; second, by disciplining myself to deliver a simple, clear message, I refine my own thinking so it is focused; and third, by communicating the message in a creative and entertaining fashion I ensure that my clients will not be able to forget it.

When people have comparable technical skills, communication ability is often the differentiator in determining who is promoted or offered more lucrative opportunities.

Many technically competent individuals discover that their own Peter Principle, or level of incompetence, is due to a failure to engage and inspire others. No matter how well educated or creative you are, you must be able to communicate your ideas effectively to have them implemented. Moreover, as people become more dependent on their electronic devices for communication, the ability to speak effectively to real humans in the same room, or online, is more important than ever.

Yet despite the proliferation of advice on public speaking, most presentations at all levels are boring and ineffective.

Why? There are two main reasons: fear and ignorance. Fear

leads many people to avoid learning how to present, thus enabling ignorance. And many people just don't know that this is a skill they can develop.

The problem with most books, seminars, and online public-speaking courses is that they focus on managing fear by orienting participants to get through their presentations without embarrassment. But if we're just trying to survive up there, our presentations will be ineffective.

When fear dominates it's hard to feel connected to an audience, and unfortunately, when we feel disconnected we are more likely to feel fear, thus perpetuating a vicious cycle.

Why is the fear of public speaking so prevalent, and how can we overcome it?

Speaking in Public: Worse Than Death?

The science section of the *Times of London* recently featured the headline "Speaking in Public Is Worse Than Death for Most." The article stated, "If you have ever thought that you would rather die than have to speak in public you may not be alone, according to a survey on common phobias. A fear of public speaking was found to be a more pressing concern than death, according to a ranking of society's most pervasive fears."

Many surveys rank public speaking as the #1 fear, greater than the fear of nuclear war, financial ruin, or getting mugged. Death ranks between fourth and seventh on a number of lists. In other words, most people would rather be resting in the casket than giving the eulogy. (Of course, when I put it that way, you'd probably be willing to give the speech!)

Glossophobia is the technical term for the fear of public speaking. And, according to the National Institute of Mental Health, 74 percent of Americans suffer from it.

Why are people so afraid of public speaking?

Glenn Croston, author of *The Real Story of Risk*, explains the primal origins of this fear: "When faced with standing up in front of a group, we break into a sweat because we are afraid of rejection. And at a primal level, the fear is so great because we are not merely afraid of being embarrassed, or judged; we are afraid of being rejected from the social group, ostracized, and left to defend ourselves all on our own. We fear ostracism so much today, it seems, fearing it more than death, because not so long ago getting kicked out of the group probably really was a death sentence."

Fear of ostracism and the potential for embarrassment and humiliation make the dread of public speaking an immediate, pressing force in daily life, often causing people to avoid public speaking altogether. Others grit their teeth and march up to the microphone like condemned prisoners walking to the gallows. Armoring themselves with glazed eyes, a frozen posture, and a monotone voice, they try to ignore, suppress, or deny their fear while cowering behind the podium. Or if they're doing a TED-style talk without a podium, they armor themselves with scripted, overrehearsed, and faux-authentic expressions of vulnerability.

The fear of public speaking is widespread, and learning to present effectively is vital for your long-term success. How can we overcome this tension? Is there some way to transform the fear into enthusiasm? Is there a way to present that feels natural, spontaneous, and even joyful for both you and your audience?

Yes! And before I take you through a proven methodology for developing those characteristics, it's important for you to know that it's okay to experience fear. The key is learning how to transform that fear into energy and enthusiasm instead of cotton-mouth and paralysis. Once you learn to use its energy, you'll realize that fear is your friend. It will keep you sharp and focused as you learn to dance with it instead of letting it bully you.

It helps to understand that many top professional speakers and accomplished actors experience butterflies in the stomach before presenting. They never eliminate the butterflies; they just teach them how to fly in formation.

Gordon Goodman, a successful actor and singer, was inspired to study the prevalence of stage fright among professional performers after experiencing it himself as he recovered from an injury that shook his confidence. Goodman found that more than 80 percent of elite professional actors experienced stage fright at some point in their careers.

Among those who have reported experiencing intense nervousness before performing are luminaries such as Adele, Rowan Atkinson, Samuel L. Jackson, Harrison Ford, James Stewart, Megan Fox, Cher, John Lennon, Amanda Seyfried, Fiona Apple, Barbra Streisand, and Sir Laurence Olivier. In other words, if you have grappled with stage fright, you are in good company!

The essential question that we will explore together is: *How do I get the butterflies to fly in formation?* Every word in this book is designed to help you transform fear and anxiety into confidence and enthusiasm.

Clarity and Presence

Before we delve into the eight secrets covered in this book, it's helpful to understand that mastering the art of public speaking is predicated on two simple ingredients for excellence: clarity and presence.

Be clear: Clarify *what* you want to say and *why* you want to say it.

Be present: Say it in the most memorable and effective way by applying the skills of presentation.

When you know *what* you want to say, *why* you want to say it, and *how* to say it, you'll discover that you feel *clear* of fear and that you are able to be fully and easily *present* with your audience.

These two words are often associated with the phrase *clear and present danger*, the title of a Tom Clancy novel and the film that followed starring Harrison Ford. The phrase was introduced to the lexicon by Supreme Court Justice Oliver Wendell Holmes in an argument about limitations to the freedom of speech. Holmes argued that the first amendment did not, for example, make it acceptable to shout "Fire!" in a theater, in the absence of smoke or flames, since this would pose a "clear and present danger."

In these pages you'll learn to protect yourself against the dangers of getting fired because of your inability to present in a theater or conference room. As Justice Holmes argued, freedom of speech doesn't mean you can or should just say whatever you feel like saying, or shouting. You must consider the context. Holmes was persuasive because he used a metaphor that was easy for people to understand, and he used it in a way that was engaging and memorable and in support of a clear, logical argument. You will learn to do the same.

Most of the problems people have when they present are a function of not preparing properly and of not being clear about what their message is and why it's important to their audience. In the simplest terms, if you don't know what you're talking about or why you're talking about it, you probably shouldn't be talking.

Once you've clarified your message, you can begin to have fun as you contemplate creative ways to present it and to make it engaging and memorable for your audience.

I'm here to tell you that you can master the art of public speaking. It is a skill that everyone can learn. Yes, some people seem to have a talent for speaking, while others often find themselves at a loss for words. Some folks yearn for the spotlight, while others avoid it. But whatever your natural gifts or proclivities, whether you are an extrovert or an introvert, you can learn the skill of presenting. In this book you'll also be guided to *unlearn* the habits you have developed that interfere with your natural brilliance as a communicator. When you were a baby, you were naturally expressive and engaging. You had charisma. As you read the pages that follow, you will begin to rediscover these qualities.

Although the steps to mastering public speaking are simple to understand, they aren't always easy to apply. Many guides to presentation suggest that you "just be yourself," as though that's a straightforward thing to do. But the "self" is multifaceted, and many aspects of it are best kept, well, to yourself. The finest public speakers cultivate this discernment so they can bring out the best of themselves in front of an audience, and that in turn leads to understanding how to bring out the best in the audience.

Authenticity versus Fauxthenticity

Synonyms for the word authentic include "original" "genuine" and "real." The word comes from the roots *auto* meaning "self" and *sene* meaning "to achieve." Presenting yourself in a genuine manner is an important element in achieving success as a public speaker. Your credibility as a speaker and leader is directly correlated with how authentic the audience perceives you to be.

Who you are communicates more than what you say.

A reporter once asked Mahadev Desai, Gandhi's personal secretary, the secret behind Gandhi's ability to enchant audiences for hours without using a script or notes. Desai replied, "What Gandhi thinks, what he feels, what he says, and what he does are all the same. He does not need notes." This is the power of inner alignment, of authenticity. Gandhi used that power to overcome his own fear of public speaking in order to change the world. And so did Thomas Jefferson, Sojourner Truth, Abraham Lincoln, Malala Yousafzai, and Winston Churchill.

Inner alignment requires inner work that many people prefer to avoid, so they fake sincerity and indulge in pseudo-authenticity. This "fauxthenticity" is on the rise, promoted by advertisers who imply that you will become a rugged individual by drinking a certain brand of whiskey or beer, driving a particular car or motorcycle, or wearing a "preferred" fashion line, watch, or necklace.

We don't develop or increase our authenticity by wearing any particular fashion or by dressing in a special way. We don't enhance it by getting a tattoo, or lots of tattoos, or by growing facial hair or shaving our heads, or by using a particular product. It's fine to express yourself any way you like, as long as you don't harm others, but being genuine isn't about external manifestations.

Wearing a particular type of outfit may be stylish and help us identify with a certain group, but it isn't a sign of ingenuity or of "keeping it real." In the words of former NBA All-Star, commentator, and philosopher Charles Barkley, "This is my new shoe. It's a good shoe. It won't make you dunk like me, it won't make you rich like me, it won't make you rebound like me, it definitely won't make you handsome like me. It'll only make you have shoes like me. Period."

Another recent trend in fauxthenticity is the liberal use of profanity, which seems to be a key to getting on the bestseller lists. Some research suggests that occasional use of profanity is perceived by some audiences as a sign of the genuineness and down-to-earth nature of the curser, but in the long term it's better to be perceived as a person who is thoughtful, intelligent, and considerate so it's best to…keep your fucking mouth shut, only kidding, I mean refrain.

To grow as a presenter, you must grow as a person.

In his classic *On Becoming a Leader*, Warren Bennis emphasizes that the quest for authenticity is the heart of leadership.
Presentations reflect your progress in this quest. To be a great
public speaker, you must learn to speak from your true self. In our
society it is not always easy to know or be yourself. Developing
authenticity, and great presentation skills, is part of a lifelong process of personal growth.

To repeat, the simple formula for giving great presentations
is be clear about what you want to say and why you want to say
it, and then to say it in an engaging and memorable way. The
most powerful presenters integrate a command of their subject
with effective, authentic self-expression. Research, preparation,
and practice set the stage for a confident, natural delivery. En-
lightenment philosopher and wit Voltaire observed, "One always
speaks badly when one has nothing to say." If you don't know
your subject, you deserve to be nervous. On the other hand, you
can't know everything. A powerful presenter and effective leader
can say "I don't know" with authority! This ability is a key to
transforming fear and inspiring confidence. How? The first secret
is to approach all your presentations like a professional presenter,
something that you will learn how to do in chapter 1.

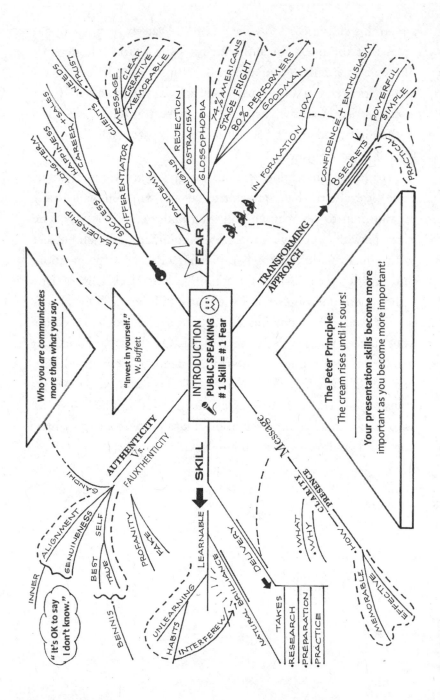

Chapter 1

In Order to Flow, Think Like a Pro

I love being a professional speaker.

Onstage, in front of hundreds or thousands of people, I experience what psychologist Mihály Csíkszentmihályi describes as *flow*. There's nothing I'd rather be doing. Time disappears, and I experience a sense of effortlessness, joy, and oneness with the audience. (Even though time disappears, I still monitor the clock because it's always important to start and finish on schedule.)

Growing up in a highly verbal Jewish Italian family, where it seemed that everyone was always speaking at the same time, I learned to put my views forward assertively. The Passaic High School senior class of 1970 voted me Class Arguer. And in 1972 my younger brother Ken received the same recognition.

Being a professional speaker has always seemed almost too good to be true. People applaud when I'm introduced. They listen intently. They applaud again, and sometimes they stand and cheer, when I take the final bow. They usually ask polite and thoughtful questions, and then they give me a big check!

I've delivered thousands of paid presentations. The shortest

13

was an eight-minute keynote at a huge corporate product launch (that was the most money I ever made per minute), and the longest was a three-week residential leadership retreat for investment bankers. I've presented to diverse audiences in more than thirty countries to groups as large as ten thousand. I love groups of all sizes. Smaller audiences allow for more direct interpersonal connection, while bigger ones generate higher energy.

Over the years, I've experienced many of the vicissitudes of the profession. My presentations have been interrupted by power failures, fire alarms, and heart attacks (not mine). I've presented within a week of major knee surgery and once with a fever of 102. I've never missed a paid engagement or been late. Once, after a delay caused by a flight cancellation, I flew all night from London to Cape Town, South Africa, arriving at 9:00 AM for an 11:00 AM keynote to eight hundred biochemists, and then I caught a 3:00 PM flight to Athens for a presentation to company presidents the next day. I've arrived to give a keynote on the same day that my client's companies announced unprecedented massive layoffs and plant closures. I've had my allotted time reduced by more than half, with less than five minutes' notice, on many occasions because of one client emergency or another. And I regularly address people who have been sent by their bosses and who are often unhappy about being ordered to attend.

Through all the ups and downs I continue to study how to connect with and provide maximum value for every group by communicating the ideas and methods that I believe will help them be more creative, innovative, and effective.

The focus here is to help you learn, in a natural, authentic, and enjoyable way, how to be clear and present when you're in front of a group or addressing them online. In the process you'll learn how to be more creative, innovative, and effective in all your communication, formal and informal, professional and personal.

Let's begin by considering a transformational secret of master public speakers. What do the pros know that most people don't?

The Professional Mindset: Thinking and Preparing Like a Pro

What's your job title?

When I posed that question to randomly selected participants in a recent seminar for the marketing and sales department of a technology company, one person answered, "Customer information liaison" and another said, "Director of marketing and retail strategy," and a third person responded, "Vice president of marketing and sales."

Here's what I said next:

From now on, when someone asks you your job title, I want you to think, "I'm the customer information liaison and a *professional presenter*," or "I'm the director of marketing and retail strategy and a *professional presenter*," or "I'm vice president of marketing and sales and a *professional presenter*."

Now, I don't recommend that you say this out loud, but I do want you to make being a speaker part of your professional identity, because your ability to be effective in any of these jobs is influenced significantly by your public-speaking skills. When you begin to think of yourself as a professional presenter, you'll start to do what professional presenters do, which is to continually study how to improve rather than just focusing on how to survive.

This secret comes first because it makes it possible to apply everything else in the book. As you adopt the mindset and then the methodology of a professional, you'll discover that your confidence, skill, and effectiveness all begin to develop together. Your expectation for yourself will create a positive self-fulfilling prophecy.

Poor speakers think of themselves as being poor speakers, so they don't prepare. They don't look for opportunities to improve or practice. They aren't mentally set to discover stories, reports, jokes, news items, and other information that could make their presentations more interesting and enjoyable. Conversely, professionals pride themselves on their public-speaking skill. They take every opportunity to practice and improve. With their minds set on success, they are always researching, generating, incubating, and evaluating ideas to enrich their presentations. Instead of running away or freezing in response to the fear of public speaking, professionals accept and embrace the butterflies.

Here are a few other simple but transformational secrets of the professional mindset.

Understanding Your Audience

Instead of worrying too much about themselves, professionals focus on empathy for the audience, understanding that they are often nervous as well.

A few years ago I was invited to give a keynote speech at a convention of eight thousand insurance salespeople. The directors of the insurance organization presented an interesting challenge: they wanted me to script my remarks and read them from a teleprompter. I explained that this wouldn't work for a presentation about innovation, which needed to be spontaneously creative. Empathizing with their need for control and reassurance, I provided a detailed outline for the presentation.

I was scheduled to be the penultimate speaker, to be followed by former First Lady Barbara Bush. The atmosphere backstage was tense, with secret service agents hovering and an expectant crowd waiting, but I was fine, practicing my centering exercises (which you will learn in chapter 7), as I always do before any significant event. Then, just as I was about to take the stage, the senior director of the insurance group approached me and, with a grim look and in a serious tone, he whispered in my ear, "Don't f**k up!" I smiled at him and reflected silently, "Gee, thanks for that timely and inspiring advice. I was planning to f**k up, but you, with that cogent and wise pointer, saved me." But then I realized that these were insurance people who are biased to control risk. I thought, "They really do need to learn how to think creatively, so let me do all I can to help them."

Professional presenters know a secret about transforming fear. In most situations, whether at a PTA meeting or a corporate conference, *the audience is nervous*. Why do you think people hide in the back row, leaving the front seats empty? Perhaps they remember the humiliation of being called on by the teacher when they were unprepared. Whatever the reason, group situations magnify the potential for embarrassment. As the speaker, you are in a position of power and control. Take care of your audience. Help them relax and enjoy your message. Direct your attention to their needs. If you focus on fulfilling the objectives you set for them, you will transform your anxiety into enthusiasm to connect with and be of service to your audience.

This attitude improves communication and encourages leadership. Paradoxically, the focus on giving great presentations becomes the key to transforming the fear that leads people to focus on just surviving.

Understanding the Art of Connection

Professionals understand that establishing and maintaining rapport with their audience allows them to get their message across and makes the whole process more enjoyable for everyone.

The professional public speaker is guided by the motto

"Connect before speaking" (*Conjungere ad orationem*). Connection, also known as rapport, is primarily a function of instinctive response. Our brains are hardwired to ask, "Is this person friend or foe?" whenever we meet someone new. As you deliver the first few minutes of your presentation, most of your audience already has unconsciously decided whether you are likable and if they are willing to be influenced by you.

Your credibility may be enhanced by the list of qualifications recited by the person who introduces you, but it is determined much more by how much the audience perceives that you are authentically interested in connecting with them and communicating something of value.

Professionals view every presentation as an opportunity to create an experience of connection with the audience. One-to-one or one-to-ten-thousand: it's all about connection. A sense of connection is the foundation of successful one-to-one communication, and it's also the foundation of successful presentations to groups of all sizes.

Many people are comfortable, and effective, speaking to one or two others, but put them in front of a group of twenty or thirty listeners, and things change dramatically. Although large groups can provide a sense of anonymity, it is a mistake to imagine that you are addressing an impersonal mass.

However large your audience, it is always individuals who receive and process your message. The greatest presenters are distinguished by their ability to make everyone in the audience feel that the presentation is being delivered personally to them.

So what does change as we shift from one-to-one to progressively larger groups? The main difference is how much you project your voice and body language to reach your audience. The larger your audience, the more you must magnify your natural movements, gestures, and vocal projection.

Making Your Presentations Creative and Entertaining

John Medina, author of *Brain Rules*, explains, "The brain doesn't pay attention to boring things." Most presentations in business and academia are boring, handicapped by an overemphasis on data, analytics, graphs, and charts. Managers, academics, and other professionals often assemble facts and then present them in a detailed, exhaustive fashion. After a perfunctory greeting, they make little effort to establish rapport, and the only food for imagination is provided by the audience themselves through daydreaming and doodling.

Of course, your message must be convincing to the rational mind (unless you are a politician or a cult leader). A great presentation is clear, concise, and compellingly logical. But logic is not enough. A great presentation captures the audience's imagination and appeals to them emotionally. As you learn to make facts come to life with stories, imagery, and humor, you'll discover that your message becomes more potent and that the process of presenting becomes less nerve-racking and much more fun.

Butterfly Alignment: Comforting Thoughts!

Here are a few comforting thoughts about your audiences to help you align your butterflies.

Most audiences want you to succeed. Inexperienced speakers often imagine that audiences are composed of rejects from *The Gong Show*, desperately yearning to wreak their revenge. In reality, most audiences are supportive. People generally attend presentations with the hope of gaining something from the time they invest. They have a stake in your success. And people tend to identify with the challenges of speaking and usually are quite tolerant of your imperfections.

Unless you are getting paid to speak, the good news is that

most audiences don't expect much in terms of presentation skill because they are used to boring and poorly delivered, unclear messages. A basic truth of life is that satisfaction is a function of expectation. And expectation is usually a function of experience. If a friend is accustomed to eating at Denny's, she will be impressed if you take her to Sizzler. If you apply the simple tools shared in this book, you will easily exceed most audience's expectations.

More good news: you usually look much better than you feel. Although you may feel nervous, the audience generally won't know it. Adrenaline causes you to exaggerate your perceptions, making you imagine that a grammatical error or an awkward movement is a massive gaffe. The audience probably never notices. Even if you are feeling shaky, you probably look fine.

So do what pros do, and *monitor your self-talk*. Learn to translate your anxiety-driven, negative inner dialogue into positive, confidence-building affirmations. When you notice the butterflies swarming, instead of thinking, "I'm so nervous about this presentation," rename the sensation "excitement." And say to yourself, "I'm so excited to present!"

In *The Sense of Style*, linguist Steven Pinker notes that many people feel as if "learning to write is like negotiating an obstacle course in boot camp, with a sergeant barking at you for every errant footfall." The advice he offers for aspiring writers is equally relevant for public speakers. He asks, "Why not think of it instead as a form of pleasurable mastery, like cooking or photography? Perfecting the craft is a lifelong calling, and mistakes are part of the game."

Like professional public speakers, you can begin to view every presentation as a wonderful opportunity to perfect your craft, learn from mistakes, and take pleasure in the journey to mastery.

Yet another secret will transform your understanding and

ultimately your skill: professionals are practicing and preparing in everyday life. Every conversation, every interaction with others, whether one-to-one or in a group, represents an opportunity to refine your ability to express yourself, to elevate your use of language, to become a better listener and a better storyteller, to cultivate the alignment of your words and your body language, and to study how your communication affects others.

For pros, this process isn't burdensome; it's fun! The truth is, there's a metadimension of learning and investigation that you can enjoy in any interaction. And even boring presentations become more endurable because as you learn these secrets you'll begin to know exactly *why* someone was boring and what they could have done differently.

In the next chapter you'll learn a simple, specific, immediately applicable professional secret that will not only transform your fear but also help you supercharge the power of your message and your effectiveness with any type of audience.

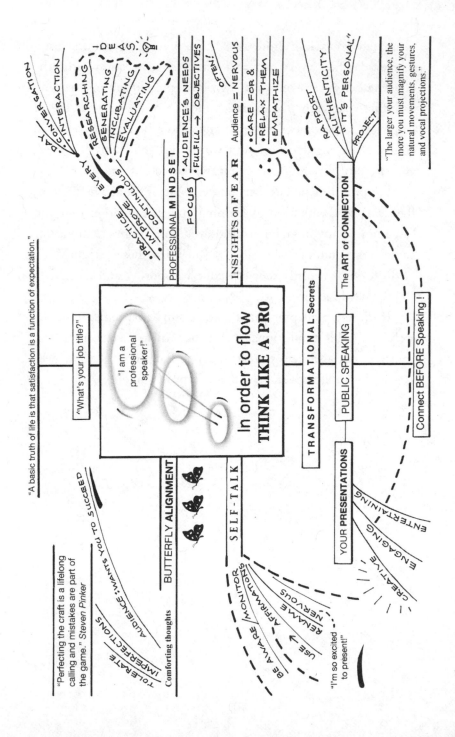

In order to flow
THINK LIKE A PRO

"I am a professional speaker!"

PROFESSIONAL MINDSET

"What's your job title?"

"A basic truth of life is that satisfaction is a function of expectation."

- **PRACTICE**
  - EVERY • DAY
    - • CONVERSATION
    - • INTERACTION
- **IMPROVE**
  - CONTINUOUS
    - RESEARCHING
    - GENERATING
    - INCUBATING
    - EVALUATING

I D E A S
- OFTEN!

FOCUS • AUDIENCE'S NEEDS
FULFILL → OBJECTIVES

INSIGHTS on FEAR — Audience = NERVOUS

- CARE FOR &
- RELAX THEM
- EMPATHIZE

The ART of CONNECTION

- RAPPORT
- AUTHENTICITY
- "IT'S PERSONAL"
  - PROJECT

"The larger your audience, the more you must magnify your natural movements, gestures, and vocal projections."

TRANSFORMATIONAL Secrets

PUBLIC SPEAKING

Connect BEFORE Speaking !

YOUR PRESENTATIONS

- CREATIVE
- ENGAGING
- ENTERTAINING

SELF - TALK

- BE AWARE / MONITOR
- USE AFFIRMATIONS
- RENAME NERVOUS

"I'm so excited to present!"

BUTTERFLY ALIGNMENT

Comforting thoughts

"Perfecting the craft is a lifelong calling and mistakes are part of the game." *Steven Pinker*

TOLERATE IMPERFECTIONS
AUDIENCE WANTS YOU TO SUCCEED

Chapter 2

Empathize with Your Audience

What is your first thought when you are asked to present? For many folks it's "uh-oh!" followed by lots of negative self-talk. Negative self-talk is associated with muscular contraction, and this contraction and tension build, leading to more worrisome thoughts and more unnecessary tension, creating a vicious, psychophysical circle of self-sabotage.

Instead, prepare your mind and body for success by catalyzing a virtuous circle of self-empowerment. This path to pleasurable mastery invites you to begin empathizing, right from the start, with the needs of the audience.

From the moment you agree to present, begin preparing yourself for success. Notice butterflies and allow them to flutter by, viewing them as indicators of excitement rather than nervousness, and *shifting your focus from yourself and onto the audience*. Invoke a sense of gratitude that people are willing to give you their attention, and become *wildly curious* about how you can best connect with them and serve their needs. Professional presenters empathize with the audience and focus on the results — the benefits — we intend to generate for them. We genuinely want to help and are grateful for the opportunity to consider and meet the needs of the people we're addressing.

After almost every presentation someone asks me, "How did it go?" I usually say something like, "Ask the audience" or "You tell me."

The great Argentinian writer Jorge Luis Borges counseled, "Don't talk unless you can improve the silence." In order to improve on silence, you need to craft your words with a purpose. Common sense dictates that when you start something, it's wise to be clear about your intention — *why* you are doing it — and the results you'd like to achieve. This is especially important in public speaking.

Clarify Your Objectives

In 1982 I moved to Washington, DC, because it seemed like a place where I could make the greatest contribution by teaching creative thinking. (Despite my tenure, there's much more progress to be made.) I arrived in DC just in time for the Redskins to win the Super Bowl, and I became a big fan. Like the Kansas City Chiefs in the 2020 Super Bowl, the team was thrilling to watch, especially in the fourth quarter, when they demonstrated an uncanny knack for coming from behind to win. In 1983 the Redskins made the Super Bowl again, and although they lost in the championship game they still demonstrated a remarkable ability to rally from adversity. After Coach Joe Gibbs left, the team's character seemed to change, and I noticed that the Redskins developed the opposite knack: they would often be ahead in the fourth quarter but then the other team would mount a comeback and the Redskins would find a way to lose. Instead of playing to win, the team seemed to be playing not to lose, using a tactic known as a "prevent defense," designed to prevent the other team from making a dramatic scoring play. The problem is that this tactic generates an attitude that doesn't tend to bring out the best.

Average and poor presenters approach speaking with a defensive attitude that prevents them from succeeding. They usually have just one objective: get through it without embarrassment. The fear of failure and embarrassment leads people to focus inordinately on themselves instead of on the audience. This survival-focused, narcissistic bias acts as a connection and communication prophylactic.

Professionals, on the other hand, play to win. We set vividly clear objectives for every presentation, and we *frame those objectives in terms of the benefits for the audience*. How will your presentation improve the lives of the people in the audience?

One of the simplest and most effective professional practices, to be used before every presentation, is to *write down your objectives* in terms of what you want your audience to

KNOW

FEEL

DO

as a result of your interaction.

Clear objectives lead to powerful messages and great results. If you set your objectives for every presentation in terms of the result you want for the audience, you will be less likely to go off on a tangent, you will find it easier to remember what you want to communicate, and you will feel much more confident. The butterflies will be directed toward a clear destination and will align in the appropriate formation.

Begin by envisioning the completion of your presentation. Empathize with your audience. Consider what's important to them.

Write out simple answers to the following questions:

What do you want your audience to *know* as a result of your presentation? Be specific. Start with a focus on *the single most important message* that you want them to understand and remember. Limit your key points to a maximum of seven. Research suggests that for most people that's the limit of short-term memory. (In chapter 4 you'll learn how to turn short-term memory into long-term learning.)

How would you like the audience members to *feel*? This question is often overlooked, especially in corporate and academic settings. One of the simple yet profound secrets of engaging audiences and selling ideas, formally or informally, is that emotion drives motion. Contemporary neuroscience makes it clear that we make most decisions unconsciously, based on our emotions. That doesn't mean that facts aren't important. The most effective presenters make compelling logical cases while recognizing that many people buy on emotion and then justify with fact. Moreover, audiences of all sizes decide quickly whether they like you, and if they do they're open to your influence, whereas if they decide they don't like you, they won't want to buy whatever ideas you're selling.

If you are setting clear objectives based on providing benefit or value to your audience, and if you genuinely care about and believe in what you are representing, then the audience will be much more apt to like you and to be open to your influence.

Before every presentation, write down how you want the audience to *feel* at the end of your talk. In other words, answer the question, "Why should this audience care about this message?" By articulating the feelings you'd like to generate, you tend to generate those feelings yourself, and we know from contemporary neuroscience that emotions are contagious, for better or worse.

Audiences mirror the inner state of a speaker. If you are bored and disinterested, the audience will feel the same. If you are enthusiastic and inspired, the audience will follow your lead.

What action do you want your audience to take? It's lovely to share ideas and to leave people feeling inspired, but the ultimate focus of most presentations is to inspire the audience to *do* something, or in some cases to get them to stop doing something. Is there something you want them to buy or sell? A behavior you want them to change? A campaign you want them to support? A petition you want them to sign?

Before every presentation, write down what, specifically, you want the audience to *do* as a result of the information you've provided and the feelings you've inspired.

If you follow the simple practice of writing down your objectives before every presentation, you'll discover that you are much more organized intellectually, emotionally, and physically.

Organize Your Nervous System

Setting objectives for the audience based on what you want them to know, feel, and do will help you organize your nervous system and make you a more effective presenter and leader. In human interactions the person with the most organized nervous system is poised to have the most influence.

Of course, to set and achieve objectives effectively, it helps to know something about your audience. The more you know, the easier it becomes to target your message accurately by using examples, stories, and key words that help the audience feel that you are speaking specifically to them.

When you are invited to speak, seek answers to these questions:

Who's coming and why?

How many people will attend?

What is their level of professional training and experience?

What is the age, gender, and cultural distribution?

What are their expectations?

Who are the decision-makers in the audience?

Are any recent events or forthcoming deadlines imping-
ing on their attention?

Have they been required to attend?

Do they have any special sensitivities, prejudices, or hot
buttons that should be avoided or approached with
caution?

Are there speakers before or after you? And, if so, what
are their topics?

Your best source for answers is usually the person who invites
you to speak. Be assertive about asking for the information you
need. In addition to the questions above, you might ask, "Is there
anything else you can tell me about this group?"

If possible, interview others who have addressed the same
audience.

Another good way to get to know your audience is to arrive early and meet some audience members before you speak. By
greeting and informally interviewing members of your audience,
you will be able to fine-tune your presentation while building
rapport in advance.

I was once scheduled to lead a seminar on memory and creative thinking for a group of auto company managers in Flint,
Michigan. I arrived early and mingled with the audience. They
told me that they had just discovered that 40 percent of them
were about to lose their jobs as the result of plant closings. With

the help of a quick Mind Mapping session, I reorganized my presentation to focus on helping them meet the challenges of this crisis.

The positive results obtained by targeting your message are illustrated in a story that bestselling author and master public speaker Harvey Mackay tells about Bernard "Toots" Shor, New York's legendary restaurateur. Apparently, Shor liked to conduct informal market research by pretending he was from out of town and asking strangers for advice on where to eat. One day, he got into a cab and asked the driver to suggest a fine restaurant.

The driver responded, "Toots Shor is the place to go. I recommend it to all my passengers, and they always love it. The atmosphere is great, the service is tops, and the food can't be beat."

As the driver maneuvered through traffic en route to the restaurant, he continued to sing the praises of the Shor establishment. As they drove up to the entrance, the thrilled restaurateur pulled out a roll of cash, peeled off a hundred-dollar bill, and handed it to the cabbie. He told him to keep the change.

"Gosh," exclaimed the driver, "thanks a lot, Mr. Shor."

KISS: Keep It Simple, Speaker

If you clarify your objectives in writing first, you'll be able to use those objectives as criteria for *what to include and what to delete from your presentation*. Delete anything that doesn't support your objectives.

A great presentation is like an iceberg: the point is clear, and the vast majority of the content is below the surface. Although professionals are always prepared with much more material than we will actually use, we always make our presentations as succinct and accessible as possible. In all the years of coaching clients on presentation, I've never suggested that anyone add more information on any of the slides in their PowerPoint.

Condensing and simplifying your material comes with two major benefits. It pushes you to a deeper understanding of your thoughts, making it much more likely that your audience will stay awake. According to the philosopher Voltaire, "The secret of being a bore is to say everything."

Many presenters suffer from the illusion that they can effectively communicate a lot of detailed, complex information in an oral presentation. This illusion was made so prevalent by the many college professors and other academics who try to prove their brilliance by making incomprehensible presentations. Perhaps this is why, in the business world, the word *academic* is frequently used as a synonym for *irrelevant*. Detailed, complex information is best communicated in writing, with a supplementary oral presentation emphasizing the key points while allowing time for a question-and-answer session.

Unless obfuscation is your aim, you will never compromise your effectiveness by simplifying your material. As the anthropologist Margaret Mead observed, "If one cannot state a matter clearly enough so that even an intelligent twelve-year-old can understand it, one should remain within the cloistered walls of the university and laboratory until one gets a better grasp of one's subject matter." The poet William Butler Yeats advised, "Think like a wise man but communicate in the language of the people."

Avoid Molecule Fondling

Many people, though very knowledgeable, aren't wise when it comes to communicating their message.

A number of years ago I had the opportunity to provide

regular seminars on creativity and innovation for chemical engineers and scientists from DuPont. The leader of this cohort invited me to work with these brilliant PhDs to help them in their presentations to the marketing and sales department. When I met with them and asked them to share their latest presentations (we recorded these on video), each scientist stood up and talked about some aspect of the molecular structure of the chemicals they were researching. It went something like this: "So we looked at the molecule under this set of conditions and we were surprised by the behavior of that molecule. We then tested the molecule under another set of conditions and once again were surprised by the way the molecule behaved."

Of course, the marketing and salespeople weren't particularly interested in the details of the specific behavior of the molecules in question. They wanted to know: What specifically will this chemical do? When will it be ready? How safe is it? And what compelling name could we give it? (After all, these are the same folks who came up with great names like Teflon and Corian.)

When the scientists watched the video, after being coached to review it from the perspective of the marketing and sales team, they all seemed to recognize that they needed to be much more audience focused. The chief scientist captured the essence of their revelation when he rose and exclaimed, "Oh, my God. We are guilty of molecule fondling!"

Almost everyone, from every profession, tends to be guilty of *molecule fondling*. The greater your expertise, the greater the danger that you will focus on the details of what you know rather than on what your audience might need. Steven Pinker refers to this syndrome as "the curse of knowledge." He explains, "Every human pastime — music, cooking, sports, art, theoretical physics — develops an argot to spare its enthusiasts from having to say or type a long-winded description every time they refer to a familiar concept in each other's company. The problem is that as we become proficient at our job or hobby we come to use these catchwords so often that they flow out...automatically, and we forget that our readers may not be members of the clubhouse in which we learned them."

We may feel that we are brilliantly articulate and persuasive, and that we make all the points we wish to make. But the effectiveness of any kind of communication, from technical instructions to words of endearment, always ultimately depends on the perception of the person receiving the message. In other words, we can't know the success of our communication unless we monitor the response of our listeners. Assume less and explain more.

Ask Transformational Questions

Professionals understand the importance of empathizing with an audience's needs. We know that if you want to connect with people, and you really want to help them, it's not good enough just to be focused on their needs in a general way; rather, you need to contemplate a question that can transform your presentation from good to great. The question is:

What is the greatest point of influence?

In other words, what factor or factors are most critical in the minds and hearts of the audience members? On what basis are they most likely to decide?

I've had the pleasure of collaborating with many clients in the construction-management industry. One of the great things about this business is that the results are evident and measurable. When you construct a building it's clear if it was completed on time, if it was done on budget safely, and of course, if it's structurally sound.

I love riding around major cities with my construction-management (CM) clients and contemplating the parts of the skyline that they helped to build. But to procure the contract to erect a building, construction managers must first give presentations to their potential clients. Most firms, universities, hospitals, and government agencies that are planning to build will ask for proposals from many construction managers before narrowing the field to three leading contenders. Then they schedule presentations by those contenders over the course of one or two days before deciding. Frequently, there's a lot at stake.

One of my clients was preparing to make a presentation to take over the construction management for a huge telecommunications company that was outsourcing this function. The CEO of the CM firm asked if I could help prepare his team for the presentation. The team was competent and put forward a strong message about all the high-quality buildings they had built, and how they were all completed safely and on schedule. It was a classic case of molecule fondling! One could be pretty sure that the competitors for this contract were also preparing presentations that highlighted their own accomplishments in regard to scheduling, budget, safety, and so on.

I challenged the team to put themselves into the minds and hearts of the committee members who would be making the decision. What, to use an engineering metaphor, might be the greatest point of leverage for winning this business? As they empathized with the potential client and considered the presentation from the client's perspective, it became apparent that they had overlooked several elements.

They realized that this telecommunications company was aiming to distinguish itself from the old monopolistic heritage of the Bell System by positioning itself as a contemporary information systems and management organization. They realized that information technology was extremely important to their potential client, and so they decided to include their IT department in the presentation. They also decided to offer a demonstration of their IT prowess with a specific focus on how they could optimize all the construction functions and track the costs of every job by coordinating with their potential client's IT team.

In carefully rereading the request for proposals, they also realized that the language included about diversity was significant. After intense discussions the team realized that they needed to address this issue because it was genuinely important to the client and not just a politically correct disclaimer inserted by their HR or legal department. In an unusual move they included their VP of human resources in the final presentation. He addressed the diversity issue, acknowledging that his industry wasn't at the leading edge. Nevertheless, he pledged to make a concerted effort to comply with the client's desire to support a more diverse workforce, and he agreed to do this whether or not they were awarded the job.

The two competitors gave presentations about quality, schedule, budget, and safety, whereas we covered those key elements and also focused on the critical points of leverage that would help the client win what was at that time the biggest contract in the history of the company.

A few weeks later, another team from the same CM firm was invited to fly to Tel Aviv to make a presentation in an attempt to win the contract to build the new airport terminal there, to coincide with a significant anniversary of the country.

Again, they were prepared to do a brilliant job of molecule fondling. Their presentation featured beautiful pictures of airline terminals that they had built, with the usual focus on their expertise in budget, safety, yadda yadda.

When I challenged them to brainstorm on the greatest point of influence for winning this business, it was obvious to the team that, in this case, information technology and diversity initiatives were irrelevant. On brief reflection it became clear that the most important factor in winning this job would be compliance with the schedule, since the members of the Israel Airports Authority probably had their jobs on the line in regard to completing the terminal in time for the anniversary.

Our team put together a presentation that featured computer-generated images of the completed airport with a digital clock readout displaying the exact date and time that the terminal would be finished. We put that image on the booklets to be handed out and also on the first and last PowerPoint slides.

I'm sure our competitors mentioned that they were good at meeting their deadlines, but we emphasized the point in a memorable way, in alignment with the highest point of influence, thereby reassuring the commission and winning the job.

Avoiding molecule fondling and focusing on the highest point of influence doesn't guarantee that you will always win in competitive situations, especially when they're complex. But it does raise the odds in your favor.

The Secret of Professional Speakers and CEOs

Legendary consultant Keith McFarland helps entrepreneurs clarify and implement the strategy they need to realize their dreams. He's discovered a surprising key to success: "It's no secret that the founders of start-ups are great persuaders who somehow manage to convince attorneys and accountants to cut fees, get vendors to offer special terms, and assure employees that low salaries now will pay off later. I call it the ability to 'recruit the world.' What is surprising is how they pull it off. It's not how you might think."

He adds, "Despite the stereotype of the hard-charging, highly critical bullying entrepreneur our research shows that successful Inc. 500 CEOs score higher than 82% of the population on their ability to express support and encouragement — higher than any other group except high-performing salespeople. They succeed by helping other people — their employees, partners, investors, suppliers — become successful themselves. In other words, they're 'Otherish.'"

The success of your presentation can only be measured by the results you achieve with your audience. If you think of your audience members as customers, you can gauge the effectiveness of your message by asking, "Did they buy it?" Successful people are intensely focused on the results they achieve with their customers or clients.

In a recent presentation to five hundred sales representatives from a hospitality company, my objectives were to be sure that at the conclusion of the hour allotted they would:

Know the five keys to giving an unforgettable sales presentation

Feel energized, enthusiastic, and confident in their ability to apply the five principles

Do by applying the five principles to measurably improve their sales performance (you will learn these five principles in chapter 4)

One of the secrets of a happy life is balancing self-awareness with focus on and care for the needs of others. The same is true for a great presentation. Nervousness can suck you into the quicksand of extreme introspection. It leads you to scrutinize and exaggerate your weaknesses, perverting consciousness of self into self-consciousness. Although healthy self-examination is useful before and after your presentation, you want to pay more attention to your audience than to yourself while you are speaking. And preparing a presentation, seminar, or speech without the objectives for your audience in mind is like writing a love letter and addressing it to Occupant.

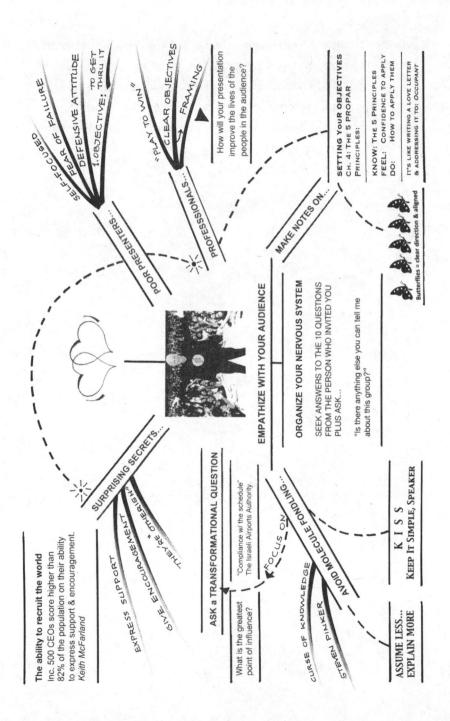

Chapter 3

Use Mind Maps to Generate, Organize,
and Remember Your Message

Once you've clarified your objectives, you'll want to come up with a creative and compelling approach to fulfilling them. And then you'll want to be sure that you remember what you want to say. When you're clear about delivering a compelling message, and you have your material well organized, you'll discover that you feel comfortable and at ease in front of groups of any size.

The most effective and enjoyable way to do this is to make Mind Maps. Mind Mapping is a method for generating, organizing, and remembering your presentation. Originated by British educational innovator Tony Buzan, Mind Mapping helps you generate more ideas in less time while making it easier to make new connections between your ideas. It awakens and enhances the more imaginative, colorful, and spontaneous elements of thought and harmonizes them with the more critical, logical, and analytical functions.

I began collaborating with Tony Buzan in 1975. Since then I've used Mind Maps to write all my books and to prepare all my presentations. I've been teaching other people how to Mind Map for more than forty years, and when I meet folks who attended one of my programs years ago, they often tell me that they are still using Mind Maps, *especially for presentations.* In this chapter I will show you how to use a Mind Map to generate and organize your ideas and then to remember those ideas. You can also use Mind Mapping as a tool for presenting your ideas in a way that is more engaging and memorable for your audience.

Beyond the Outline

Louisa, a project manager at a large corporation, must lead meetings and give presentations as a regular part of her job. For many years she found this to be an almost unbearable undertaking. Her main problem was her difficulty in generating and organizing ideas. Although she was knowledgeable in her subject area, she often found that when she sat down to prepare a presentation, her mind would go blank.

Like most of us, Louisa was trained to generate and organize her thoughts in a step-by-step, linear manner, using an outline. As we all know, an outline begins with roman numeral I. Louisa would sit at her desk for long periods of time, waiting for idea number I. After what seemed like an eternity, she would get an idea and proceed from there.

She would often find, however, that when she got down to, say, III C, it should really have been II A. She would start crossing out and drawing arrows, and suddenly realize that her neat outline had become a mess. Sometimes at this point she would begin doodling or daydreaming, but that made her feel guilty that she wasn't being productive, so she would try to concentrate on the right order, and this often resulted in more frustration.

Louisa is not alone. For many people the process of preparing a presentation is fraught with frustration, anxiety, and discarded ideas.

Why? Frequently it's because we expect ideas to emerge in a linear fashion. But for most people, thinking just doesn't work that way.

Think about the last book you read, the last TED Talk you watched, or the last meeting or seminar you attended. Imagine that you have to write a report or give a presentation on that book, talk, meeting, or seminar.

Begin recalling the information. As you do, observe the process of your mind at work. Does your mind work by constructing complete sentences or whole paragraphs or by presenting ordered outlines? Probably not. Chances are that impressions, key words, and images float into your mind, each one associating with the next. Mind Mapping is a method for continuing this natural thinking process on paper, or on the computer.

Outlining is valuable as a tool for representing ideas in a formal, orderly fashion, but *it is useful only after the real thinking has been done*. If you try to generate your ideas by outlining, you will find that it slows you down and stifles your freedom of thought. It is just plain illogical to try to organize your ideas before you've generated them. An outline reflects a hierarchical mindset that cauterizes creativity. Outlining and other linear note-making systems exclude your brain's capacity for color, dimension, synthesis, rhythm, and image. By imposing one color and one form, outlining guarantees monotony. Outlining uses only half of your mind, and the other half of a mind is a terrible thing to waste!

Mind Mapping: Streams of Development

Mind Mapping is based on the confluence of the following streams of research and understanding.

Studies of Note-Taking Skills

In the late 1960s Tony Buzan worked at the College of Advanced Reading in England, where he taught speed-reading and study skills to students while researching methods for improving learning, memory, and creative thinking. He did an extensive study of various note-taking styles, aiming to discover what would work best for his students.

Drawing on the research of Professor Michael Howe at Exeter University, Buzan concluded that the best notetakers shared two distinctive characteristics. First, they used key words. Key words are the nuggets of creative association and recall. They are information rich. When you think of a key word, it inspires other key associations.

For example, if you are familiar with Shakespeare's *Hamlet*, and I ask you to think of some key words associated with the play you might think *tragedy, Denmark, prince, Ophelia*, and so on. Examples of nonkey words might include *the, and, of,* and *so*. Once you've learned grammar and syntax, your mind automatically knows how to place key words into sentences. Nonkey words aren't necessary for recall, so you don't need to include them in your notes.

Howe's other important finding was that the best notetakers keep their notes clear and easy to read. Many students suffer from an inability to read their own handwriting, making their note-taking efforts useless. Howe observed that the best notetakers took the time to print their notes rather than to write in cursive. Printing, in addition to making the notes easier to read, *imprints* the key thought more clearly in the mind of the notetaker.

Mind Mapping originated as a tool for both note-taking and note-making. Note-taking focuses on recording someone else's thoughts, as from a book, lecture, seminar, or meeting.

Note-making is for generating, organizing, and integrating your own thoughts and for fully incorporating the thoughts that you've learned through note-taking into your thinking process.

Mnemonics and the Psychology of Memory

The Greek goddess Mnemosyne was Zeus's consort and the supreme deity of remembrance. The word *mnemonic*, a mental strategy for enhancing recall, comes from the same source as her name. Mnemonics can be used to improve your ability to remember almost anything, from randomly shuffled decks of cards and digits of pi, to names, anatomical information, and, of course, material for oration. The ancient Greeks developed mnemonic systems to help them remember the content on which they based their oratorical contests. Buzan made an intensive study of mnemonic systems and, along with chess grand master Raymond Keene, created the World Memory Championships.

Mnemonics are based on two key elements of recall: association and emphasis. You remember things because you *associate* them with something else, and the Greeks noticed that imagery, color, and other sensual elements created more *emphasis* and that this made associations more memorable. In a Mind Map you use key words, images, and color to make your notes for your presentation much easier to remember.

An Understanding of Networks and Natural Systems

Contemplate the structure of a tree; it is a network of life, expanding in all directions from its trunk, its center. Take a helicopter ride over a major city; it is a sprawling structure of interconnecting centers and pathways, main arteries connecting with side roads. Our global telecommunication systems and the internet are similarly linked networks. The structure of communication in nature is nonhierarchical and self-organizing; it works through networks and systems. The ability to read, align, and work creatively with these systems is ultimately the definition of intelligence.

The most amazing system of all is right inside your skull. The basic structural unit of brain function is the neuron. Each of our billions of neurons branches out from a center, called the nucleus. Each branch, or dendrite (from *dendron*, meaning "tree"), is covered with little nodes called dendritic spines. As we think, electrochemical information jumps across the tiny gap between spines. This junction is called a *synapse*. Our thinking is a function of a vast network of synaptic patterns. A Mind Map is a graphic expression of these natural patterns of the brain.

An Understanding of What Great Minds Do

The note-taking styles of many of history's great brains such as Charles Darwin, Katherine Johnson, Thomas Edison, Marie Curie, and Leonardo da Vinci feature a networked, branching structure, along with lots of creative doodles, sketches, and key words. Mind Mapping integrates and formalizes what the creative mind naturally wants to do.

The Rules of Mind Mapping

The rules of Mind Mapping are all based on the information we just reviewed about effective note-taking, the nature of memory, observation of nature, a practical understanding of the structure and design of the human brain, and study of the thinking patterns of great brains.

1.   **Begin your Mind Map with a symbol or a picture at the center of your page.** Starting at the center rather than at

the top of the page helps to free you from the limitations of hierarchical, "top-down" thinking. It opens your mind to a full 360 degrees of associations. Pictures and symbols are much easier to remember than words and enhance your ability to think creatively about your subject. Your drawing will serve as the home base for your creative associations. Don't worry if you think you can't draw; just do the best you can. You can get the brain benefits without being a Leonardo da Vinci or a Georgia O'Keeffe.

2. **Use key words.** Key words are the information-rich nuggets of recall and creative association. They are easier to remember than sentences or phrases. We can generate key words faster than sentences or phrases, without sacrificing meaning. Moreover, training yourself to look for key words enhances your ability to get to the essence of your material.

3. **Connect the key words with lines radiating from your central image.** By linking words with lines (branches), you'll show clearly how one key word relates to another. Connect the lines for maximum clarity.

4. **Print your key words.** Printing (rather than writing in cursive) makes what you write easier to read and remember.

5. **Print _one_ key word per line.** By doing this, you free yourself to discover the maximum number of creative associations for each key word. The discipline of one word per line also trains you to focus on the most appropriate key word, enhancing the precision of your thought and minimizing clutter.

6. **Print your key words on the lines and make the length of the word the same as the line it is on.** This maximizes clarity of association and encourages economy of

space. (You will need plenty of space because you will be generating ideas faster than ever!) Avoid letting your key words float off the lines. This graphic disconnection short-circuits the flow of association.

7. **Use colors, pictures, dimension, and codes for greater association and emphasis.** Highlight important points and show relationships between different branches of your Mind Map. You might, for instance, prioritize your main points through color-coding: highlighting in yellow the most important points, using blue for secondary points, and so forth.

    Use pictures and images, preferably in vivid color, wherever possible; they stimulate your creative association and greatly enhance your memory. Codes, such as asterisks, exclamation points, letters, shapes, and numbers, can be used to show relationships between concepts and to serve as tools to further organize your map.

8. **Free-associate, then organize.** The process of making a Mind Map to prepare a speech or presentation is divided into two major phases. The first focuses on generating as ideas many as you can in as short a time as possible. In this *free-association* phase, simply let your mind go, and write down as many key words and images as you can. Even if a word seems ridiculous or irrelevant, put it down and keep the process flowing.

    After you have generated a wealth of associations, you will begin the second part of the process: the *organization* phase. Here you will examine your map from a more analytical perspective, eliminating those elements that now seem superfluous and consolidating your key concepts. You can use numbers, additional colors, letters, or other codes to impose a clear sequence on your material. In some instances, you may wish to redo your map in order to organize it further. At this stage you might, for example, put your first point at one o'clock and proceed accordingly, in a clockwise rotation. You may even choose to translate the map into outline form, now that you've clarified your ideas.

Mind Mapping Your Presentation

Mind Mapping is easy. It doesn't demand much — just your brain, a few colored pens, a piece of paper, and a willingness to learn something new. Although Mind Mapping is used in a wide variety of applications, including strategic planning, academic study, and creative problem solving, it is particularly helpful in presentation design and delivery. Try making a Mind Map to help you prepare for your next presentation. Use the following points to guide you.

(*Important note:* Although many software programs have evolved to do Mind Mapping, you will get much more benefit from the method if *you first learn it the classic way — by hand*, with colored pens and a large sheet of blank paper. I call this artisanal Mind Mapping.)

To begin, get a large sheet of plain paper — preferably white, and the bigger the better — and five or more colored pens. Phosphorescent highlighters are also useful, since you can read through them. (One pen and a small sheet of paper will still work in a pinch, however.) Place the paper horizontally on a table or desk in front of you.

Having identified the topic for your presentation, draw an image that represents it in the middle of the paper. It doesn't matter what the image is, or whether it is abstract or concrete, as long as it reminds you of your topic. Draw it as vividly as you can, using at least three different colors. Have fun, and don't worry about the accuracy of your drawing.

Next, look at your sketch and start printing key words on lines radiating out from your central image. Remember to print on the lines, one key word at a time, and keep the lines connected. Use pictures and colors whenever possible. Let your associations occur spontaneously, and fill the page as quickly as you can. If you run out of room and the ideas are still flowing, get another piece of paper and keep going. If you get stuck, choose any key word on your map and immediately print your first association with that word, even if it seems irrelevant. Keep your associations flowing, and don't worry about getting every word "right."

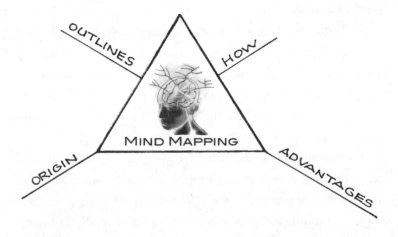

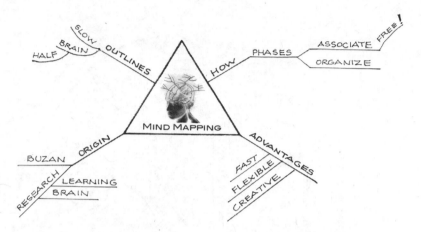

When you feel you have generated enough material, take a look at the result: all the ideas for your presentation spread across one page. Having given your imaginative mind the spotlight as the generator of these ideas, shift focus and use your analytical mind to put your map in order.

As you look at your map in this more analytical way, you will begin to see relationships that will help you organize and harmonize the presentation you are planning. Look for words that recur throughout your Mind Map. They often suggest the major themes that will integrate the different aspects of your talk.

Connect related parts of your map with arrows, more lines, codes, and colors — whatever works best for you. Eliminate anything that now seems extraneous. Pare down your map to the ideas you need for what you're going to say. Then put these ideas in sequence. If necessary, redo the map to make it neater and easier to follow.

Although many people, especially those who feel trapped in the need for premature organization, can benefit from just jotting down lots of ideas in a webbing-, spider-, or bubble-diagram format, applying all the rules of Mind Mapping will prove to be much more useful over time.

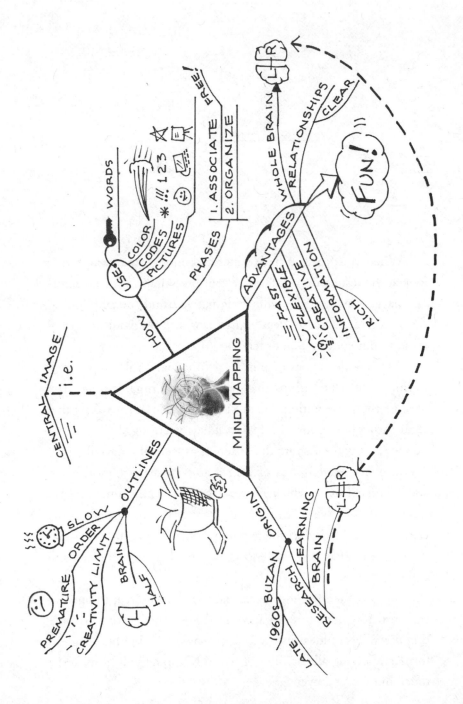

In his forty years in the construction management industry, Jim D'Agostino has led the successful completion of a range of iconic projects, including the Los Angeles City Hall, the Four Seasons Hotel & Residences, Aquarium of the Bay at Pier 39 in San Francisco, and the Grand Central Terminal revitalization in New York City. Jim notes that Mind Mapping has been an indispensable tool in his career:

I was exposed to various alternative note-taking methods like webbing and spider diagrams, but I found them disjointed. Then I learned Mind Mapping in a seminar with the author when I was chief operating officer of a major New York firm many years ago. Since then I've been Mind Mapping everything! I remember when I first learned about starting at the center and using images and key words. It really liberated my thinking. Mind Mapping has helped me develop as a strategic and creative thinker.

When you're working on huge, complex projects there are innumerable concerns and endless details that require attention. In other words, there's a lot that can go wrong! Mind Mapping makes it much easier for me to see the big picture and the details. And now that I run my own construction consulting firm, I use it with my clients to map out projects in a way that literally helps us develop a shared vision. I've also found it to be particularly useful in preparing and delivering presentations. Success in this business demands an understanding of architecture, engineering, finance, and many other technical elements, but more than anything else, this is a business based on connecting and communicating effectively with all kinds of people, from laborers to developers. The ability to craft a clear message and get it across in a way that gets people to buy in may be the most important skill in construction management, and Mind Mapping makes that easier and more fun to do.

Jim's story is one of hundreds that I've been privileged to be part of through learning about Mind Mapping and teaching it to many clients over the years.

The Advantages of Mind Mapping

Mind Mapping offers many advantages over the other techniques commonly used to organize ideas. For starters, it gives you easier access to your creative power. It allows you to start quickly and generate more ideas in less time. Its free-ranging format — adding words to one branch one moment, then skipping over to another branch the next — increases your chances of generating new ideas. Mind Mapping lets you develop a logical sequence and detailed organization of your material while encouraging imagination and spontaneity.

Mind Mapping allows you to represent a tremendous amount of information in a relatively small space. You can have all your notes for a topic on one piece of paper, with your ideas arranged in a way that encourages you to see relationships between them. Mind Mapping helps you see connections among things that previously may have seemed completely unrelated. It gives you a clear view of both the details and the big picture of your subject.

Mind Mapping integrates the convergent aspects of our mind's functioning — logic, language, mathematical reasoning, attention to detail, sequence, ordering, and analysis — with the more divergent elements — dimensionality, rhythm, color, pic-tures, symbols, imagination, and synthesis. Mind Mapping "res-cues" those elements previously relegated to the realm of doodling and daydreaming, making them a productive part of our thinking and problem solving. Our minds work best when we discover a dynamic balance between convergent and divergent thinking. I call this *synvergent thinking*, a neologism I introduced in 1994. (*Synvergent* uses the prefix *syn*, meaning "with" or "together," and refers to the synergy generated when we integrate these modes of the mind.)

Mind Mapping is the simplest, most efficient way to develop synvergent thinking. How? Mind Mapping *creates a positive feed-back loop*. Our notes are manifestations of our thinking. If we manifest our thoughts in harmony with the natural functioning of the mind, we think better. In other words, Mind Mapping works by creating a positive feedback loop between your brain and your notes. Mind Mapping trains you to manifest your thoughts in a way that makes it easier to see the whole picture and the details, to integrate logic and imagination, art and science. By allowing you to capture a large amount of information on one piece of paper, Mind Mapping helps you see the relationships, connections, and patterns of your ideas. Regular practice of Mind Mapping trains you to think in a more creative, systems-oriented manner. And it's fun! It encourages creativity and humor in the process of develop-ing a presentation. This in turn leads to a more lively and engaging delivery.

Remembering your material also becomes much easier. Col-ors, images, and key words, three central ingredients of Mind Maps, are much more engaging to the brain than sentences. A well-made Mind Map is almost impossible to forget.

Here's a simple and effective technique guaranteed to help you remember the material for your presentations.

Use codes, colors, and symbols in your Mind Maps.

The Mind Map Memory Method

Although it's fine to bring notes with you when you make your presentation, it is best to emancipate yourself from your dependence on them. If you have made a clear and vivid Mind Map to prepare your presentation, you are one step ahead, since imagery, color, and key words make Mind Maps easy to remember. Then, to make sure that you remember it, take out a new sheet of paper and re-create the map from memory. When you have finished, check it against the original map, and fill in anything you may have left out. You will find that if you follow this re-creation process two or three times, the material will become etched in your memory. To enhance your memory further, pin the map to a wall, close your eyes, and practice re-creating it in your mind's eye.

Open your eyes, and check it against the original. Do this until you can re-create the entire map effortlessly. Two or three times should be sufficient.

Through Mind Mapping, you can start to infuse your presentations with more life, creativity, and fun. Yet no matter how good you become at generating and organizing ideas, your presentation must be designed with your audience in mind. Ultimately, all that matters is what your audience understands and retains.

In the next chapter, you'll learn methods for ensuring that your audience receives your message and remembers it.

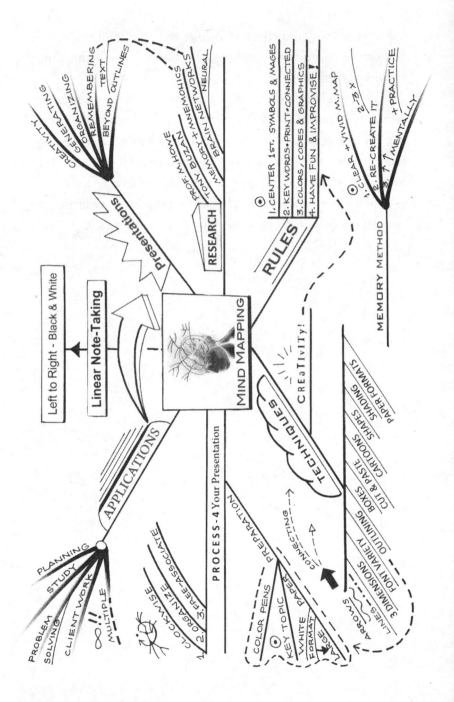

Chapter 4

PROPAR

Structure Your Presentation So That the Audience Remembers Your Message

H ere's an excerpt from an email I received recently:

> When I was relatively new in the business, I attended
> your keynote on Leonardo da Vinci at a divisional con-
> ference way back in 2002. I've just been asked to lead
> a group here at my company, and we're responsible for
> driving an innovation effort for our department. Can you
> help us?

I confess that I'm not (yet) a master of social media or
email marketing. Fortunately, throughout my career I have focused on making my presentations memorable and on connecting
with people. The result is that most of my clients are now direct
referrals from someone who heard me speak, sometimes many
years ago.

When I first started speaking I thought the most important
goal was to get people to understand my message, but I soon

realized that *understanding was necessary but not sufficient.* Understanding must be complemented with *remembering.*

Why? Because they are two different phenomena, and not necessarily correlated.

Understanding versus Remembering

No matter how well prepared and poised you are when speaking, your presentation is only effective if your audience *remembers* what you want them to remember. This is not as obvious as it sounds.

A common pitfall in communication is confusing understanding with remembering. Your audience may nod in apparent understanding, but that does not mean that they will remember your words. Of course, remembering without understanding would not be useful either.

To really understand this point and make it more memorable, please take this 101-word memory test. Ask someone to read the list to you, or just read it once without going back over previously read words. Then write down the words you remember. Ready? Go!

auspicious	control	read
record	maid	Oprah Winfrey
mitten	opposite	Oprah Winfrey
throw	public speaking	Oprah Winfrey
speak	haircut	honey
dance	shock	hushed
honey	robust	aggressive
vest	cub	tub
cover	big	powder
improve	inflate	tea
sample	lean	fast

mature	sniff	cope
public speaking	limping	knee
wide	build	reduce
note	nest	show
gifted	condition	honey
test	purify	cakes
shoot	bird	coherent
draw	ignite	apologize
counsel	fish	public speaking
fame	lie	swim
mother	honey	pray
honey	kneel	own
middle	dispensable	cooperative
obscene	wind	possessive
bereave	army	honey
goldfish	festive	hear
bomb	button	wanting
abashed	approach	wonderful
public speaking	draw	warn
let	sniff	auspicious
fans	parts	record
date	kid	mitten
loud	trip	

How many words did you remember?

Did you remember *auspicious*, *record*, and *mitten*?

Oprah Winfrey?

honey?

public speaking?

Most people remember the above words.

Auspicious, *record*, and *mitten* are the first three words on the list and the last three words as well.

Oprah Winfrey's name was repeated three times in a row, and it was the only proper name on the list.

Honey was repeated five times.

And, *public speaking*, of course, is the subject of this book.

Five Principles That Organize Recall

As our memory exercise illustrates, five principles organize recall during a presentation. They are primacy, repetition, outstandingness, personal association, and recency, or PROPAR. This acronym will help you remember the principles of remembering!

We tend to remember what comes first. First impressions really are significant. Psychologists call this the *primacy effect. Auspicious, record,* and *mitten* were more memorable in our test because they came first. We also tend to remember the last thing that happens in any particular sequence, and *auspicious, record,* and *mitten* showed up again at the end. The tendency to remember the last thing is called the *recency effect.* Unless you're a trained mnemonist, you tend to forget the words in between the beginning and the end of the list. The exceptions are words that are repeated. Repetition makes things memorable. Allow me to repeat: Repetition is memorable. Right, honey? We also remember anything that is outstanding, and besides being an outstanding person, Oprah Winfrey is the only proper name on our list. We also remember anything that has a special personal association, so for example, you are reading a book on public speaking so that phrase probably stayed in your memory, enhanced further by its repeated use and by its outstandingness, in that it was the only phrase on the list.

What are the five principles that organize recall during a presentation? Just remember PROPAR! Primacy, repetition, outstandingness, personal association, and recency.

Consider the average presentation. What parts of it are you

most likely to remember? Most people would say the beginning and the end, and they're right. People tend to remember the first thing that a speaker says and, if they're still awake at the end, the last. And in many cases they forget just about everything in between.

How can you take advantage of the primacy and recency effects and raise your audience out of the trough in the middle?

By using these five principles of recall. Taken together, these principles form a simple and powerful strategy for making your message unforgettable. Effective communication requires the integration of understanding and recall. The PROPAR approach holds the secret of that integration. Let's look at how to apply each element.

The Primacy Effect

If your colleague comes into the office on a Monday morning and says, "We are going on a trip," the first question likely to come to your mind would be, "Where are we going?" Once the destination is known, your next question might be, "Why are we going there?" You'd probably follow that with, "How are we going to get there?"

A presentation is a journey of communication. An audience wants to know where you plan to take them, why they should go with you, and how you are going to get them there. So, in the first few minutes of your presentation:

Make contact with your audience. If your colleague is a skilled communicator, she will take time to establish personal contact before announcing the trip. A simple, sincere, "Good morning, how are you?" accompanied by natural eye contact, sets the stage for cooperative action. It is the same when you are presenting to a group.

In 1980 Tony Buzan and I led a three-day seminar for five hundred children in Soweto, South Africa. On the first morning, I walked onstage and said, "Good morning." The children, who were used to being taught by rote, responded with a lifeless, "Good morning, sir." So I said, "No, you didn't understand me, I really mean it. GOOOOD MORNING!" A constellation of smiles appeared before me as five hundred giggling children, their minds and hearts now open to learning, howled, "GOOOOOOOOOOOOOOOOD MORNING!" When we connect with an audience at the beginning of a presentation, we set the stage for ease, flow, effectiveness, and memorability. Sometimes this can be challenging.

I recently gave a keynote speech for an audience of more than a thousand people in Ankara, Turkey. The speaker before me was a senior government official who went well over his allotted time and, although he was speaking in Turkish, it wasn't difficult to discern that he was a boring presenter. When he finished, the emcee went to the podium and introduced me in Turkish. As I walked onstage the government minister and his entourage of about twenty people sitting in the front two rows stood up and shuffled out. I waited for them to depart, and when they had all filed out I paused for a moment, looked out at the audience, and said, "*Merhaba*" (Turkish for *hello*). The audience applauded, and we were now connected. Here's what I said next:

> I want to tell you about a miracle that happened on my way here. When I flew from Albuquerque, New Mexico, to New York City on an American air carrier last week, I wasn't served anything that any of us would call food. After a few days in New York City I flew to Rome on an Italian air carrier, and I have to say the food was disappointing. But yesterday I flew from Rome to Istanbul and

was served a delicious meal on Turkish Airlines. Then we had to change planes for the short flight from Istanbul to Ankara, and this was the real miracle. We were served another amazingly delicious meal on the short flight. Slow-cooked lamb and imam bayildi (which means "the imam (priest) fainted" and is a yummy eggplant dish). Wow. Thank you, Turkish Airlines!

Yes, Turkish Airlines was the sponsor of the event. And it doesn't take too much research to learn a simple greeting in Turkish, and you don't have to be a scholar of Turkish culture to know that food and hospitality are important. Saying hello in Turkish created a positive primacy effect, and as I told my story the group relaxed and we connected, and they were open to my message.

Once you connect with the audience, let them know where you're going and how you're going to get them there. Communicate your key points in the beginning. And frame your key points in the context of *benefits for the audience*. As you clearly relate your message to the audience's concerns, you capture and keep their attention.

If your presentation is longer than twenty minutes it's a good idea to give an overview. When you share the structure of your presentation, you mentally set the audience to remember your message. When you show them the path you'll be traveling, they will be much more willing to accompany you.

I recently gave a keynote speech to a group of nine thousand at the Future Medical Leaders conference in the hockey stadium at the University of Massachusetts at Lowell. When I walked out from behind the curtain, I saw that the crowd was wedged up around the edge of the stage, and it looked like a rock concert with a perfect takeoff area for a stage dive and crowd surf. I spontaneously ran forward and pretended that I was going to jump out into the crowd! Then I asked, "Will you catch me?" and the audience cheered and laughed. Now we were connected and in rapport. My topic was *How to Think Like Leonardo da Vinci*, the title of a book I released in 1998. Here's what I said next:

> *Buona sera* [Italian for "good afternoon/evening"]. When I was a child Leonardo da Vinci was my hero, along with Superman. I remember when I discovered that Superman was only a comic book character, but Leonardo da Vinci was real. The more I learned about him the more amazing he seemed to be. I went to the place he was born. I went to the place where he died. I literally walked in his footsteps and looked at the world from his point of view. I read his notebooks over and over again and visited the great museums of the world where I contemplated his masterpieces. I interviewed the great da Vinci scholars. All this with a question in mind: What can we learn from him? What's he trying to teach us? I started dreaming about him. And from those dreams, seven principles emerged.

Then after a bit more background I completed the introduction by saying, "We are going on a journey into the mind of the greatest genius who ever lived. At the end of this talk, you will be able to draw on the wisdom of Leonardo to help you in your greatest life challenges. You'll learn his approach to being more creative and living a more beautiful life. Are you ready?" (Audience cheers and affirms their enthusiasm.)

I share these examples to inspire you to think about how you can take advantage of the first few critical minutes of your presentation — the primacy effect — by connecting in your own most authentic way with your audiences and then by delivering your key message in the framework of the benefits for them.

Repetition

A great myth about communication is that if you say something and your audience seems to understand it, they will remember it. If you want your audience to remember your message, *you must repeat, you must repeat, you must repeat* it. Tell your audience what you are going to tell them. Then tell them. And then tell them what you told them. Many of the finest speakers pause and review their key points as they make them.

Of course, intelligent use of repetition requires avoiding monotony. Use visuals and other creative means to reinforce your points. A creative and effective approach is to find a phrase that summarizes your message and rhythmically repeat the words in the manner of Dr. Martin Luther King Jr. ("I have a dream") or Muhammad Ali ("I am the greatest").

Be sure to repeat all your key points. I once shared the stage with a speaker who was trying to generate support for a new educational program. In his enthusiasm for this project he repeated the phrase "It can be done!" innumerable times in twenty minutes. His passion and commitment were unquestionable, and the audience was clearly energized. Later, I asked someone what the speech was about. He replied, "I'm not sure, but whatever it is, we can do it!" So be careful and intentional about what you repeat.

I sometimes speak to groups about improving the brain as we age. Most people don't know this is possible. One of my main objectives when I speak on this topic is to open the audience's mind to this notion: *Your brain is designed to improve with use.* I present plenty of scientific evidence and engaging stories to support this contention. And depending on the amount of time and the particular interest of the audience, I then focus on *the best ways to use it in order to improve it.* When the audience enters the room they see the phrase *Your brain is designed to improve with use* on my PowerPoint slide, or on a flip chart if it's a smaller, less formal presentation. I repeat the phrase multiple times throughout the presentation, and my goal is that if you ask someone what they learned in my talk they will say, "I learned that my brain is designed to improve with use." Followed by "and I learned the three most powerful ways to use it in order to improve."

And a special magic takes place when we share and repeat our message in three key words or phrases, known as triads. Roman orators were inspired by the maxim *Omne trium perfectum*, which means "Everything that comes in threes is perfect." From Julius Caesar's *"veni, vidi, vici"* ("I came, I saw, I conquered") to Steve Jobs's introduction of the iPad 2 "thinner, lighter, faster," the thoughtful use of the triad makes your message memorable.

Outstandingness

If you want your audience to remember your message, you must make it outstanding or unusual, and the easiest way to do this is to tell a story. Do you have any tchotchkes — odd, random objects also known as trinkets, gewgaws, baubles, curios, or miscellaneous junk in your home? The kind of stuff that just seems to accumulate over the years? Have you ever considered selling any of it at a yard sale (or on a contemporary electronic version of a yard sale)?

About ten years ago journalist Rob Walker purchased two hundred items like this on eBay for an average price of less than $3 per item. Then he contacted the same number of authors and asked each writer to craft a fictional story about one of the objects, creating something like an online J. Peterman catalog for knick-knacks. Playwright Neil LaBute wrote about a candle shaped like a bunny rabbit. LaBute's "Rabbit Candle" story is short and captivating and includes these words: "I knew the truth — perhaps

I alone — that it was made of real gold and that there was an actual bunny buried deep inside the wax.... One day, if I was very good...we would light it together and set the bunny free." The Bunny Candle, purchased by Walker for $3, sold for $112.50. In many cases items accompanied by stories — and it was always made clear that the stories were fiction — were sold right next to the same item without the story. The storied items outperformed the nonstoried items by almost 3,000 percent!

A well-told story dramatically enhances how your audience perceives the value of whatever you're selling. And it isn't just more engaging for the audience; it also engages the storyteller, making it easier to deliver a presentation in a more natural and stress-free manner. Over the years many of my clients who started out with paralyzing stage fright discovered that the surprising secret to overcoming fear was to craft and deliver outstanding stories and creative demonstrations.

One of those clients, an internal corporate pension investment fund, set themselves the goal to become an independent business. To accomplish this they first had to convince the corporation's pensions and benefits committee to give them operational control of the company savings plan, which at the time was under the stewardship of an outside firm. The director of the fund challenged each of his team members to generate a compelling story or demonstration that would convince the committee that his team had a better understanding of their investment philosophy (they were value investors) than the outside firm and that they could manage the investments in a more cost-effective way.

In our strategy session it was clear what we wanted the audience to *know*: we understand value investing better than the competition. We can manage the money in a significantly more cost-effective way. We wanted them to *feel*: a sense of comfort with and trust of our team. And it was vividly clear what we wanted them to *do*: transfer control of the assets and ultimately let us spin off our enterprise.

Each team member designed and delivered a presentation involving a story or demonstration that helped make these points. Steve, the group's director of venture investments, was, like most of the team members, an introverted analytical thinker who was initially uncomfortable as a public speaker. But motivated by the desire to fulfill the team's dream of being an independent enterprise, he rose to the occasion. Steve helped close the sale by convincing the board that the savings plan was an undervalued asset that would be better managed under his group's stewardship. After greeting the board members and giving them a brief overview, he tossed a handful of nickels, dimes, and quarters onto the boardroom table, right in front of his boss's boss's boss. He asked, "How much is the change on the table worth?"

The board members counted up the coins. One of them said, in an impatient tone of voice, "One dollar and fifty cents. So what's the point?" We had prepared Steve for this moment and he paused, rose to his full stature, smiled, and said: "May I respectfully suggest that you examine the coins more carefully?" At which point one of the board members, the company's chief financial officer, noticed that one of the quarters was silver. He exclaimed, "Well, this one here is silver, and we don't see those very often these days; it's probably worth five or six times its face value." Steve then handed that gentleman a magnifying eyepiece and suggested an even closer look.

"Wow," exclaimed the CFO, "this coin has an unusual mint mark and is also an antique. This is a rare coin worth many times its face value! Where did you get this?"

Steve paused and then after passing the rare coin around so that everyone could see it and touch it, he collected the change and put it back into his pocket. After another well-timed pause he said, "This quarter [borrowed for the occasion] is just like our savings plan, an undervalued asset just sitting in our pocket. Let me show you how we can take better advantage of it." He then took them through the numbers and made a logical, compelling case. His presentation made the value message unforgettable, and his poise in presenting it built a sense of confidence, trust, and connection that captured the audience's attention and ultimately control of the $7 billion savings plan.

Demonstrations, stories, humor, and drama are especially important in more technical, complex, and detailed presentations. More than just entertainment, a well-told story raises your audience's attention, engagement, and retention. *The key is to link the story to the most important point you want people to remember.* In the case of the pension fund, the link to the surprise discovery of a silver quarter and the message of an undervalued asset was simple, immediate, unforgettable, and effective.

Neuroeconomist Paul J. Zak, a professor at Claremont Graduate University explains why storytelling is so important: "My experiments show that character-driven stories with emotional content result in a better understanding of the key points a speaker wishes to make and enable better recall of these points weeks later. In terms of making impact, this blows the standard PowerPoint presentation to bits."

Zak adds, "I advise business people to begin every presentation with a compelling, human-scale story. Why should customers or a person on the street care about the project you are proposing? How does it change the world or improve lives? How will people feel when it is complete? These are the components that make information persuasive and memorable."

The key to making this work is to find, as Steve did, a story, demonstration, metaphor, or joke that feels natural for you to share. This is one of the reasons it's so important to think of yourself as a professional presenter, because it's just natural for professionals to look for these kinds of stories in the flow of everyday life.

Personal Association

You are chatting with a friend at a party when suddenly you hear your name being spoken across the room. Until that moment, you had heard only a general din. But now your attention is captured. This is the power of personal association.

People hear and remember things that are relevant or meaningful to them. They tune out and forget things they don't care about. Having tailored your message to be relevant to your audience, you must now deliver it in a manner that maximizes their involvement.

Steve's silver coin presentation was dramatic and outstanding, but the other secret of its success was his skill in getting his audience involved. By throwing coins on the table and asking engaging questions, he transformed his audience from distant judges to co-explorers of his work.

How can you maximize audience involvement? The simplest way is to ask questions, both real and rhetorical. Did you know that asking an audience a rhetorical question dramatically raises their attention and recall levels? If I ask you about something you are interested in, what does it lead to? Thinking, participating, connecting, and forming personal associations.

Take every opportunity to get your audience involved. Try beginning a presentation by inviting the audience to engage in a task, test, or challenge related to the message. This instantly brings them fully into the present moment and into the role of cocreator. For example, in my presentation on improving the brain with age I usually ask the audience, "Is anyone here over thirty?" I raise my hand, and then many in the audience raise their hands. Then I ask, "Anyone under thirty?" Hands go up. Now everyone is involved. Then I ask, "What happens to your memory as you approach, or pass, age thirty?" People are now answering this question in their minds, usually with some idea that memory declines with age. The presentation continues with a series of rhetorical questions, followed by evidence-based answers and then a memory quiz in which the average score is 4 out of 10. This is followed by about ten minutes of coaching on how to improve memory, which is then followed by another memory quiz in which the average score improves to 10 out of 10. In other words, instead of just presenting the data on the possibility of memory improvement, I invited the audience to experience improving their memory, making the data much more meaningful and memorable.

So whenever possible, create a context, through the use of exercises and questions, that allows the audience members to discover the message for themselves.

The word *education* comes from the root *educere*, which means "to draw forth" or "to lead out." However, many of us were raised in an environment in which *educere* might have meant "to stuff in." As a presenter and leader you are responsible for guiding the process of drawing forth, not stuffing in.

The Recency Effect

As your presentation draws to a close, you have one last opportunity to achieve your objectives — to make certain that the audience knows, feels, and does what you want them to know, feel, and do. Now you must "close the sale." As Henry Wadsworth

Longfellow emphasized, "Great is the art of beginning, but greater the art is of ending." And comedian Jerry Seinfeld observed, "The biggest laugh has to be at the end."

Repeat your key points (review your overview), and issue a call to action. Even better, maximize personal association by asking your audience to review the main points and to explain how they will apply what they have learned. If appropriate, ask participants to make a specific commitment to applying their new knowledge.

The recency effect applies not only to content but also to emotion. Great presenters finish strong, building energy to a positive climax. End on a high note. Many speakers sabotage their recency effect by going on too long. Discipline yourself to finish on time, or a bit early. It's always better to leave them wanting more rather than wishing the presentation were over.

The Power of PROPAR

The PROPAR principles are always operating, consciously or unconsciously, and for better or worse. The "for worse" happens when speakers create a *negative primacy* by beginning their remarks, for example, by apologizing for not having enough time to prepare or by unskilled self-deprecation: "I'm not really qualified to speak to such an esteemed audience." Then instead of repeating a carefully crafted key message, they repeat *um, ah, like,* and *you know* over and over again. So later when someone asks, "What did you get from that presentation?" they respond, "Um, ah, like, you know, I'm not really sure." When the message of a presentation isn't made outstanding in some compelling way, it's all too easy for audience members to forget, especially if they don't feel engaged personally through questions, exercises, or stories and examples. Boring, forgettable presentations often end with a negative recency when speakers finish by apologizing and self-deprecating again at the end: "I'm sorry we didn't get to cover all the material. Thank you for bearing with me, and thank you for your time."

To understand the power of PROPAR, consider the strategies employed by the high-stakes communication of advertising. What happens when you are watching television and a commercial comes on? The colors on your screen get brighter and the volume gets louder, a primacy strategy designed to prevent you from muting or channel surfing.

On the internet you've probably noticed that whenever you look up something, targeted ads start appearing everywhere you go, repeating product names incessantly. Why? Market research shows overwhelmingly that many people buy purely on name recognition. And based on your overall search history and the algorithm's analysis of your likely buying preferences, you'll be presented with enticements designed to target, via careful personal associations, whatever your perceived weakness, fear, or desire may be. If the algorithm thinks you're single, you'll get dating ads tailored to what it is programmed to calculate are your preferences; if it thinks you're old, you'll get incontinence, erectile dysfunction, and assisted-living ads.

But despite the increasing sophistication of electronic seduction, old-fashioned media still works, too. On route 95, outside Wilmington, Delaware, stands a huge billboard with just two words on it: BUD LIGHT. The billboard has no pictures of ecstatic models or messages extolling the product's virtues. Just those two words. People on their way to work drive past it day after day. Anheuser-Busch knows that simple repetition of its product's name will result in greater consumption.

Advertising and public-relations firms wage a continual war to find new ways to implant their clients' products in your brain. They capture your attention and your business by making their message outstanding.

Many advertisers make their message outstanding by exploiting sexual desire. Seductive models, both male and female, hawk everything from beer, coffee, and cigarettes to health clubs, deodorant, and toothpaste. Advertisers rely on creating the following conversation in their audience's minds: "Me see sex, me see product...me want sex, me buy product."

Some of the most sophisticated commercials emphasize personal association. Companies like McDonald's and AT&T specialize in creating heartwarming, deeply human scenarios that reach out and touch their audience's wallets. And all major companies engage in targeted marketing, tailoring their message to varying demographic profiles, pandering as shamelessly as possible to whomever they think might buy more of their stuff.

And how do commercials end? Usually with one last repetition of the name or phone number, or with a close-up of a celebrity's head, just centimeters away from the product. Sometimes they conclude with a call to action — "Text us now!" "Click on this link for massive free stuff forever" "Pick up your phone and call now" — accompanied by an attractive model texting, clicking, or punching in a number, just in case any viewers forgot how to make a phone call.

Why do advertisers spend billions using PROPAR principles to create commercials that are often moronic and insulting? Because these ads are effective. PROPAR works, whether we like it or not. It can be used for evil or for good. Hitler, Stalin, and Mao, as well as Churchill, King, and Gandhi all intuitively applied the PROPAR approach.

Please use PROPAR for good and to protect yourself from being manipulated by evil. In our media-intensive age, advertisers, politicians, and social and religious groups are waging a constant battle for your mind. Use your understanding of these principles to keep your mind free and flexible as you develop your gifts as a presenter and leader.

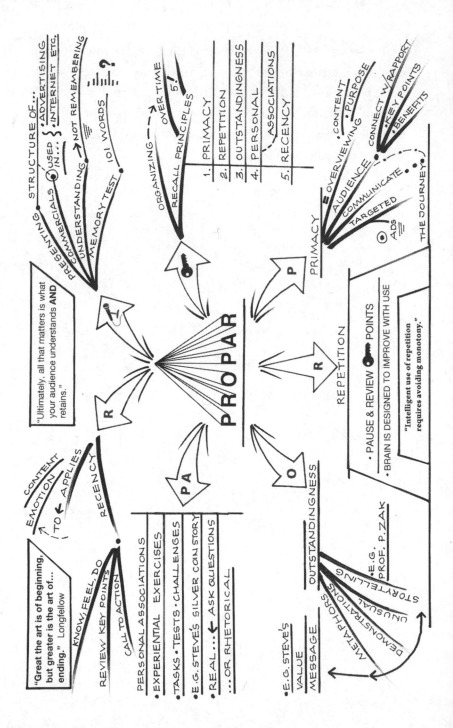

Chapter 5

All Business Is Show Business

The PROPAR principles determine what we remember, or forget, whether it's an advertisement, a sales presentation, or a meeting to enroll people in a campaign to clean up the local wetlands. These principles are also the secret of theater — and all public speaking, including business and academic presentations, are theater, for better or worse. All business is show business.

Set Your Stage

A few years ago, I was invited, on two days' notice, to speak at a conference for the external-affairs and public-relations division of one of the world's largest telecommunications companies. The purpose of the conference was to build support for a new advertising strategy, which included moving the company's entire mega-million-dollar advertising budget to a new agency. The conference slogan was "You'll Take Us There!"

The company rented the grand ballroom at a luxury hotel and spent a fortune on mock-ups of the new ad campaign. They provided a comprehensive, beautifully produced handout and first-class refreshments. I was offered my full fee to speak for eight minutes on "Meeting the Challenge of Change."

Arriving early to get to know my audience and check out the environment, I discovered that the seating and stage arrangement was a setup for disaster. The audience of more than four hundred people was to be kept in the dark, as spotlights focused on corporate honchos perched on a dais that seemed as high as Mount Olympus. The speakers were scheduled to make their presentations from behind enormous podiums. I also discovered that the podiums had control buttons, allowing speakers to adjust their height.

Although management aimed to deliver a message of inclusion, empowerment, and inspiration, the audience was likely to feel alienated, distanced, and patronized.

I quickly Mind Mapped a new slant on my presentation and consulted with the lighting and stage crew. I took a seat at the back of the darkened ballroom and awaited my turn to speak. After being introduced, I strode briskly up the center aisle (in the dark), leaped onto the stage, and stepped behind the podium. Like the speakers who preceded me, I projected nothing more than a talking head.

I started, in a monotone voice, to talk about change and the pressure and anxiety it creates, and how anxiety can create barriers between people when they need to find a new approach to collaboration. As I said the word *barriers*, I pressed the Up button, and as I continued to drone on, the podium rose and I slowly disappeared from view. Unseen for about fifteen seconds, I expounded without pause on the challenge of change and its effects on communication.

Then I leaped out from behind the podium and in an expressive, energizing voice I emphasized the importance of moving beyond barriers. Standing in the spotlight, I urged the audience to recognize their power to make a difference — to create the kind of corporate culture they wanted. As I emphasized the theme of self-empowerment, the spotlights shifted to focus on the audience, and they exploded in spontaneous applause.

Use your environment to empower your message, and be sure that it doesn't sabotage your presentation. As philosopher Marshall McLuhan said, "The medium is the message." The environment in which you make your presentation sometimes communicates more strongly than your words. You probably won't need to make the dramatic alterations that were required in my presentation, but you can increase your effectiveness by mindfully setting the stage to create a better experience for your audience.

The lighting, air quality, even the shape of the room — along with many other factors, including your appearance and the audiovisuals you're using — can have a profound influence on your audience's ability to enjoy and remember your presentation and on your sense of confidence and comfort as the speaker.

Stand-up comedy is probably the most challenging form of public speaking. Jerry Seinfeld, a master of the art, explains that the environment, the physical context, is a "gigantic aspect" of success or failure, stating, "The room is doing 80 percent of the job." The ambiance of the space, the sight lines, and the lighting and acoustics can work either for you or against you, and professionals know the importance of adjusting them accordingly. Always consider these factors to make the most of your presentation environment.

Space, Ambiance, and Furniture

Always aim to give your presentation in a room that provides ample space for every member of your audience. Set up the chairs — and tables if necessary — in an arrangement most suited to the kind of presentation you are giving. For groups of about twenty-five people or fewer, a U-shape design is most effective, since it encourages maximum interaction and participation. For larger groups, a modified classroom-style arrangement is recommended.

Whatever seating arrangement you choose, always remove empty chairs from the room, or at least move them to one side. Vacant seats are a distraction and can unconsciously draw the audience's attention away from your message. Remove other unnecessary objects as well, such as charts or audiovisual equipment left over by a previous speaker. If there are whiteboards behind you with messages written by previous presenters, erase them before you begin.

Set up the room and furniture so that they're conducive to connecting with your audience. Before you begin speaking, put yourself in the audience's position, literally: sit in the back row and imagine what it's going to be like to participate in your presentation. If you're presenting virtually, be sure to view your "stage" from the audience's perspective and create a background that makes it easy for people to enjoy seeing you on their screens.

Many presentations are delivered in drab, generic rooms. Dull environments tend to have a dulling effect on the minds of audience members. Whenever possible, create a livelier, more attractive space. A bouquet of fresh flowers and a few well-placed green plants can transform a space aesthetically and will enliven and engage your audience, thus making them more receptive to your message.

Also consider air quality and temperature. Most presentations are given in rooms with poor ventilation, and often the rooms are either too hot or too cold. Stuffy air can lull your audience into a sleepy state, and an uncomfortable room temperature is a constant distraction. Aim to give your presentation in a well-ventilated room with a temperature of approximately 68 degrees F. The air quality and temperature can often be modified through the judicious opening and closing of doors and windows. If ideal temperatures cannot be met, it is better to err on the side of the room being too cool.

Lighting

Just as it's often too cold or too warm in the room, it's also frequently too bright or too dark. My preference is for more illumination — you don't want to keep the audience in the dark, literally and figuratively. If you're speaking at a large event, practice onstage beforehand with the spotlights on, because they can be blinding and quite disorienting if you're not ready for them. Also check for reflected light that might create a glare that interferes with your visuals.

Podiums and Lecterns

At many presentation venues, it is just assumed that the speaker will use a podium or lectern, which gets placed right in the center of the stage or riser. I recommend having it moved to one side or the other, and then it's fine to begin your presentation from that base. If you stay there throughout, as many people do, it's harder to connect with the audience, who are likely to perceive you as a "talking head." Practice emerging from behind the podium and interacting with your audience. You can keep your Mind Map notes and glass of water at the podium and use the podium as a base, but learn to be independent of this unnecessary barrier between you and your audience.

Music

Music can help engage the audience's attention and uplift their energy. Experiment with what works best for you. A few of my favorites include the overture to Mozart's *Marriage of Figaro* or Vangelis's "Chariots of Fire" for the walk onstage, Glenn Miller's "In the Mood" during breaks, and Handel's "Hallelujah Chorus" or Beethoven's "Ode to Joy" for the finish. Even if you're not able to have these tunes played for the benefit of everyone, you can always craft your own pre-presentation playlist to help get you in the mood and to orchestrate your butterflies.

Each of these elements of setting your stage may seem peripheral to the effectiveness of your presentation, but when you add them together they can make a big difference. Although there are occasions when it is difficult to manipulate the environment in the manner I have suggested, you will be surprised at what can be accomplished if you are focused and insistent. Whether you are giving a presentation within your own organization or coming in from the outside, you can almost always create better conditions. Ultimately, everyone will be glad you did.

Create your own environmental checklist in preparing for presentations, and send it, well in advance, to whomever is in charge of the arrangements. Follow up with a phone call, and review each item. Arrive early enough to check the details and make any last-minute changes.

Here are a few more things to take into consideration when setting the stage.

Appearance

When I first started as a professional speaker, business audiences wore, and expected a speaker to wear, attire that was much more formal than it is today. One of my first major investments was a hand-tailored suit made in London's famous Savile Row. It served me well for years. I remember when suit and tie gave way to business casual and have witnessed the shift from casual Friday to casual every day. Nevertheless, your appearance is still your most powerful visual, and audiences will judge you by yours. Despite the trend, especially evident in online videos, toward demonstrating how authentic one is by dressing like one just rolled out of bed, most audiences in a professional context still scrutinize every detail of a speaker's grooming and dress. Is your blouse the wrong size? Are your shoes unshined? Is your nose ring too big? If you are not sure, at the first break, slip into a restroom stall, have a seat, and listen to the conversations around you.

To avoid becoming the subject of negative restroom reviews, and to be sure that your appearance doesn't distract from your message, heed the following advice.

Dress and groom yourself so that you feel comfortable and confident. When in doubt, err on the side of being more formal and conservative.

Wear clothes that fit well, in colors and fabrics that are complementary to one another and to you.

Pay attention to detail. Shine your shoes, iron your shirt (even if it's a T-shirt), use a lint brush on your jacket. Look your best, and enjoy it.

Be slightly better dressed than your audience. Although they seem to be getting more casual every year, most professional and corporate organizations are still hierarchical and a bit like the military. If you are with a group of majors and you wear the uniform of a corporal, they'll send you out for coffee. Dress like a colonel, and they'll salute.

Cultivate your own sense of style. If you can, find a few outfits that make you look and feel great, and consider wearing them just for presentations. Enjoy looking your best, and let your clothes become part of your aura of excellence.

Before you walk into the meeting room, auditorium, or virtual set, make it a habit to check your appearance in the mirror or monitor. If you had a spinach salad at lunch and one of your teeth is now green, that will be all the audience talks about when you're done. Tie everything designed to be tied, tuck in whatever needs to be tucked, zip everything that's meant to be zipped.

Master of Mind Mapping and internationally renowned public speaker Brian Weller shares a story that highlights the importance of this last point.

> When I was twelve years old, Benjamin Britten, the great composer, selected me as a soloist for the premier of his *Saint Nicolas* cantata, to be performed in front of a thousand people at Wigmore Hall in London.
>
> During the intermission, I went to the men's room, and to my horror discovered that my fly was open! Had the audience noticed? I experienced intense panic, shaking involuntarily and crying uncontrollably. The feelings were overwhelming and terrible, but I knew I couldn't run and would return for the second half of the concert. I had no choice but to let the fear run through me completely, and then something extraordinary happened. The emotional storm clouds passed, and I felt a deep sense of relief. I zipped my fly, took a deep breath, and walked back onstage. The concert was a big success. Although I didn't speak about my breakdown for many years, as you can imagine, I always check my fly every time before I speak in public!

There's more to Brian's story than just a reminder to zip up before getting onstage.

With the wisdom of hindsight, and with many years of professional presenting now behind me, I'm able to put this incident into perspective. I discovered, by serendipitous accident, that being present with fear is the secret of transforming it. My stormy emotions were so strong that I had no choice but to surrender, letting my anxious thoughts "fly" through me. I was then graced with a sense of freedom that allowed me to recover and give my full attention to singing and being with my audience. This experience opened my curiosity about the nature of mind and how being present makes all the difference in performance and in life.

Audiovisual Aids

Appropriate use of audio and visual aids can dramatically improve the impact, efficiency, and memorability of meetings and presentations. Test and practice with PowerPoint, flip charts, and videos before using them. Make certain that visuals can be clearly seen from all parts of the room.

Use audiovisuals to highlight and emphasize the *key points of your presentation*. Whether you are using a flip chart, PowerPoint, or any other medium, do not try to fill it with too much detailed information. Your audience will almost never be able to follow information presented in this way. Apply the KISS principle, making all your visuals simple and clear. Follow Margaret Mead's advice — if an intelligent twelve-year-old couldn't understand your visual, don't use it.

Audiovisuals are powerful tools for capturing the attention of an audience. Use them consciously. Be certain that your audience is seeing *only* what you want them to see, when you want them to see it.

You must be the primary medium for delivering your information. So please don't rely on audiovisual aids to do the work for you. Avoid hiding behind audiovisuals, or speaking to them. Your job is not to disappear in the dark while the audience looks at slides or a video, or to talk to your flip chart. If you do, you may lose your rapport with your audience — and the impact of your presentation will suffer.

If you plan to use complex audiovisual equipment, practice with it beforehand and learn its operational ins and outs thoroughly. Nothing will be more distracting to an audience, or potentially damaging to the impact of your presentation, than if you're fumbling with your equipment onstage. *Always be prepared for the possibility that your equipment will fail* or that materials you requested will not be delivered.

When using electronic media, check the wiring on the floor and be sure you won't trip on it! Professional AV teams will usually tape it carefully so that this doesn't happen, but always double-check.

Now let's consider how to make the most of some commonly used presentation tools.

PowerPoint, Keynote, and Other Tools

Slides can have tremendous impact, and they also have entertainment value. If you plan to use slides as part of your presentation, remember these few simple points: think carefully about how each slide supports your objectives, and show the minimum number of slides necessary to illuminate each of your points. You can almost always improve on a slide presentation by eliminating or simplifying slides. Use images and key words instead of sentences and paragraphs. Show pictures that are *worth* a thousand words, not pictures *of* a thousand words.

Use a remote-control device to advance the slides, allowing you to move freely and to interact with your audience. Always check beforehand to be sure that the slides are upright, focused, and in the correct order.

Video and Film

Video and film can be the most engaging and entertaining of audiovisual tools. They are so powerful, however, that they can often obscure the role of the presenter. They are best used as a substitute for a stand-up presentation rather than as a complement to it. So when using these media, bear in mind that you are functioning primarily as a facilitator and discussion leader.

Flip Charts

Flip charts are readily available, portable, and easy to use. To make the most of this medium, you must *print* legibly in large, bold letters, using different colors. Use key words or phrases rather than sentences. Flip charts are good for drawing diagrams, graphs, and other pictures that illustrate your key points. Chart sheets should be uncluttered and easy to read. When appropriate, prepare your flip chart before your presentation, although sometimes you will want to write or draw as you go. Write on every third sheet to prevent the audience from reading through the partially transparent paper.

Only use a flip chart in a relatively small group. Sit at the back of the room before you begin your presentation to test its legibility. Flip chart sheets can be awkward to turn, making it difficult to refer to previous sheets. You can overcome this by using multiple charts and by removing the sheets from the easel and hanging them on the walls.

Handouts

Handouts are an effective way for you to provide more detailed information to your audience. It's usually best to let your audience know that you will give them supporting materials at the conclusion of your presentation. Avoid distributing handouts at the beginning of the presentation, or your audience may focus more on the handout than on what you have to say. The exception is if you are going to refer specifically to a handout, in which case you'll need to distribute it before you do so. Direct your audience to the relevant part, giving them time to read it. When they have finished, ask them to put the handout aside.

Microphone

Use a microphone only when necessary. Amplified sound is often distorted and difficult to modulate. It is vital when using a microphone that you become comfortable with the amplified sound of your own voice. Always test the microphone before you begin speaking, and if you are inexperienced, take some extra time to practice. If you are using a standard microphone, aim it at your mouth, from a constant distance of six to eight inches away. Whenever possible, use a cordless collar microphone to allow maximum freedom of movement and more consistent voice modulation.

Timing

In Switzerland and Germany, audiences expect events to begin and end *exactly* on time. In Latin America and Italy, a more casual approach to timing is the norm. Wherever you go, be prepared to start on time but also ready for the start to be delayed. Finish on time or a bit early because it's always better to leave people wanting more than to go on too long.

When giving longer presentations, give your audience breaks. Many people complain that they don't like to give breaks because it's hard to get people back in the room, but that's usually because presenters who don't give breaks tend not to be engaging, and the audience never knows when they may get another break, so they luxuriate in the one they were given. Moreover, decades of research into what psychologists call the "reminiscence effect" make it clear that appropriate breaks enhance learning and recall. In a daylong presentation, a group that gets a ten-minute break every hour will remember more, and rate the session better, than a group that isn't given breaks. Breaks influence what people remember, and they also help to regulate energy, so the group that gets a break every hour will feel much better at the end of the day than the group that is not given breaks. It's best to give breaks before they're needed, preferably at a high point of energy and attention. This creates a positive recency effect and leaves your audience wanting more, and when they return you can repeat or emphasize one of your key points to take advantage of the new primacy effect you have created by giving the break.

The Introduction

A primacy effect is created before your primacy by the person who introduces you. Whenever possible, arrange to have the most senior, authoritative person available do the introduction, and be prepared with a Mind Map of what you would like her to say. Ask her to keep the introduction brief, under two minutes, and encourage her to create an environment of expectation and interest. Three main things can go wrong with the introduction:

The introducer reads your bio verbatim in a monotone voice.

The introducer hallucinates that he is the featured speaker and blathers on, cutting into your time.

The introducer mispronounces your name and makes a series of inaccurate statements.

If possible, engage the introducer in a conversation about why they invited you to speak so the intro can be delivered more like a story, and if necessary, help them craft objectives in terms of what they want the audience to *know* about you, how they want them to *feel* about the presentation, and what they want them to *do*.

Before the formal introduction is made, be sure that all questions concerning the availability of toilets, refreshments, and other basic needs are answered. Basic needs dominate human attention. If people are thirsty or if they need the restroom and don't know where it is, they will not be focusing on your message.

If you set your stage appropriately, you will preempt most distractions. Nevertheless, from time to time, you may be confronted with inoperative or noisy HVAC systems, exploding projectors, jackhammer choruses from the street, or bomb scares. Whatever the distraction, acknowledge the problem with good humor and act with common sense. Strange as it seems, if a speaker fails to call attention to a continuing distraction, an audience tends to blame the speaker for it.

Along with applying the PROPAR principles and setting the stage, public speakers need to embrace yet another element of theater, one that will help them transform their fear and master their art.

Rehearsal

You can craft a brilliant message focused on what you want the audience to *know*, *feel*, and *do*; you can organize it around the PROPAR principles so that they will never forget it; and you can carefully set your stage so that the environment is conducive to success, but if you don't remember your presentation when you are in front of the room, then all your other efforts will have been in vain.

Here are a few simple and effective ways to ensure that you will remember your presentation:

Begin with a positive attitude and visualization, reframing butterflies as "excitement."

Apply the Mind Map memory method. You may also wish to have your Mind Map in sight for a quick reference when you are giving your presentation.

Practice sharing your presentation with a friend. Become comfortable expressing your message in a natural, conversational way. When I'm getting ready for a new presentation, I usually ask my wife if I can share what I'm planning to say as we are driving in the car or sitting on a train.

Then give your presentation to a friend or colleague (or spouse) in a more formal way. Practice with any audiovisuals or props you intend to use. Become fluent in whatever medium you intend to employ. Do this a few times first without asking for any feedback so you can get comfortable with the content and flow, and then ask for constructive criticism.

Next, make a video of one of these sessions. Watch the playback from the perspective of your prospective audience, and ask friends and colleagues for constructive feedback. For particularly important presentations, ask them to play the role of a critical, disruptive audience, to be devil's advocates and point out any possible weakness in your material or delivery. Although this experience may be somewhat unsettling, it will prepare you ably for your actual presentation — which should be easy by comparison.

Time your practice sessions. Become familiar with the amount of time it takes to cover your key points, and bear in mind that your actual presentation will probably take longer than it does in rehearsal. Set minimum and maximum times for each branch of your presentation. Anticipate the effect of questions and inter-ruptions on your timing, and always have more material available than you actually need.

Use your visuals to help you remember. On flip charts you can leave yourself reminder notes in pencil that only you can see, and a well-crafted PowerPoint serves as a memory device for the speaker. In larger, more formal presentation venues, you'll often be provided with a "confidence monitor" that shows you the slide that your audience is seeing and your next slide; you can easily create this for yourself in less formal situations on your own lap-top or mobile device. If you apply all the elements of rehearsal we've covered, you probably won't need this, but it is nice as a backup.

Rehearsal is about more than just remembering. As you prac-tice delivering your message, you'll develop and refine it. Acad-emy Award–winning actor Sir Ben Kingsley explains that the quality of the event the audience experiences is "largely deter-mined by the rehearsal process and the experiments that you go through and the choices that you make in the rehearsal room, not in front of an audience."

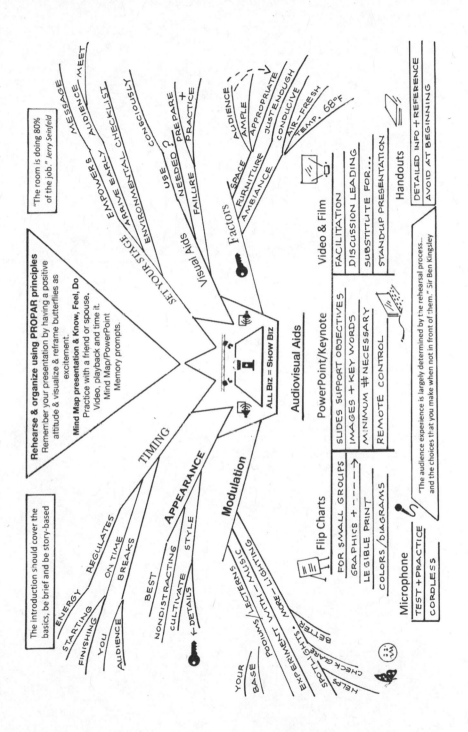

Chapter 6

Words Matter

Parisian Jesuit Dominique Bouhours was a linguist and grammarian whose last words are the apogee of passion for precise language: "I am about to — or I am going to — die; either expression is correct." Bouhours's devotion to clear usage may have been extreme, but attempting to be a public speaker without a knowledge of and feeling for words is like trying to be a chef without caring about the quality of your ingredients.

A master chef will insist on using only the freshest ingredients while employing the sharpest knives. A speaker on the path to mastery will discard rancid clichés and slice away habitual interjections in order to serve her audience fresh, sharp turns of phrase.

In the kitchen the quality of fish, meat, and produce affects the digestibility and tastiness of the meal. In the conference room or auditorium, the words you use will make a difference in the effect you have on your audience, producing either confusion and indigestion or clarity and nourishment.

Professional speakers delight in finding just the right word, phrase, or metaphor to express what we wish to say, and we understand that skill with words reflects and supports clear thinking.

One of the simplest and most powerful secrets behind effective public speaking is continually refining your ability to speak well by bringing attention to words and using them effectively.

Here are three ways to improve your skill with words:

1. Eliminate the inessential.
2. Develop your vocabulary.
3. Listen to great speakers, and read great writers.

Let's take a look at each of these concepts.

Eliminate the Inessential

The difference between being perceived as a thought leader and being thought of as a moron is often a function of what you choose *not* to say. When you use clichés, habitual interjections such as *like, you know,* and *um,* and when you speak in jargon that your audience doesn't know, you are communicating a lot about your intelligence, character, and empathy. Although every now and then one can justify sharing a well-chosen expletive, repeating curse words doesn't strengthen your case, make you more authentic, or enhance the way others perceive you.

Avoid Clichés

Lack of originality, expressed through the overuse of meaningless or uninteresting phrases, is energy depleting to both you and your audience. If you allow your speech and writing to be dominated by clichés instead of articulating what you want to say in your own words, you will dull your mind and compromise your authority. Consistent effort to use lively, clear language will help you cultivate creativity and authenticity while avoiding mindlessness and mediocrity.

As French wordsmith Gérard de Nerval observed, "The first man who compared a woman to a rose was a poet, the second, an imbecile." Novelist Martin Amis emphasizes that to write well one must declare a "war against cliché." He notes, "All writing is a campaign against cliché. Not just clichés of the pen but clichés of the mind and clichés of the heart. When I dispraise, I am usually quoting clichés. When I praise, I am usually quoting the opposed qualities of freshness, energy, and reverberation of voice."

The same is true for speaking. Clichés are a substitute for thinking. Overreliance on hackneyed phrases dulls your wits.

Here are a few examples heard both recently and repeatedly over the years:

"Here's a download of awesome life hacks."
"Let me run it up the flagpole to see if everyone buys in to the notion that this is low-hanging fruit."
"I have limited bandwidth and I'm basically out of pocket this week, so let's circle back; ping me and we will sync up so we can take it to the next level."
"To be perfectly transparent, at the end of the day, it is what it is."

These phrases, and many like them, have become ubiquitous.

Eliminating clichés requires self-awareness and vigilance. When you notice that you are about to use a hackneyed phrase, pause for a moment and think about what you really intend to say.

For example, instead of: "Here's a download of awesome life hacks."
You might say: "I'd like to share some exciting ideas to improve your quality of life."

Instead of: "Let me run it up the flagpole to see if everyone buys in to the notion that this is low-hanging fruit."
You might say: "I'd like to consult my colleagues to see if they agree that we can accomplish this with minimal expense and effort."

Instead of: "I have limited bandwidth and I'm basically out of pocket this week, so let's circle back; ping me and we will sync up so we can take it to the next level."
You might say: "I'm sorry, but I'm too busy this week. Can we please arrange something for next week? I'm excited about working together."

Instead of: "To be perfectly transparent, at the end of the day, it is what it is."
You might say: *Nothing.*

When asked, "Is sloppy communication due to ignorance or apathy?" legendary columnist, linguist, and wit William Safire quipped, "I don't know and I don't care." If you do care and you do want to know, then keep these questions in mind before you speak:

What precisely do I intend to express? (And asking "what?" implies that there's a "why" — an intelligent reason for your expression. Or as forensic linguist Tammy Gales asks, "So what? Why should I care about what you're saying?")

Is there a simpler, clearer way to say it? Thoughtful and persistent contemplation of these questions will guide you to clarify your thinking and discover your own wellspring of originality. When you free yourself from the habitually unoriginal use of language, you discover your true wit.

But, like, you know, I wouldn't get too wound up about clichés. Don't sweat the small stuff! For all intents and purposes, clichés are kind of like business as usual, if you know what I mean. Frankly, when push comes to shove, on a level playing field, they're par for the course. When it comes to meaningless drivel, at the end of the day we will have come full circle, but of course if you hope to take your speaking skill to the next level, that is neither here nor there.

Overusing clichés isn't a sin, but it's also not a cause for admiration. As the fellow who couldn't pronounce "Armageddon" commented, "It's not the end of the world."

Speakers on the path to mastery cultivate awareness of clichés and become sensitive to the effect words have on their audiences. Some expressions are notorious for the negative response they generate. Here are ten of the worst.

The Ten Most Annoying Expressions in the English Language

Inspired by the Oxford University list of the top ten most irritating phrases, and by humorist Brandon Specktor, who has compiled a similar ranking for *Reader's Digest*, here are my nominations.

10. **It is what it is.** Everything is what it is. Perhaps some people say this in a feeble attempt to convey an existential perspective. There's a whiff of a Niebuhrian, Zen-like sentiment here, as though the user would like to say, "It's important that we accept the things we can't change." A darker interpretation is offered by the *Urban Dictionary*, which interprets it as a euphemism for a sense of resignation and helplessness in the face of seemingly unchangeable circumstances.

9. **At the end of the day.** This one was used seven times in a recent segment of ESPN's *SportsCenter*. A weak substitute for other anemic phrases such as "When push comes

to shove" or "In the final analysis" or "When all is said and done." One of the *Urban Dictionary*'s top definitions is "Rubbish phrase used by many annoying people." The only legitimate usage of "at the end of the day" is when you are referring to something that takes place at dusk. Otherwise, discard this twaddle. Ultimately, you're better off using the word *ultimately*.

8. **At this moment in time / In this day and age / In the current climate.** These are all vapid ways to say "now."

7. **Honestly / Candidly / Frankly / Let me be frank / Let me be transparent.** Using any of these implies that the speaker is making an exception from their customary practice of dishonesty, obfuscation, and corruption.

6. **Thanks in advance / Thank you for your time.** The first is often used as a euphemistic, corporate way of saying "Do this or else." If you mean "I would be grateful if...," followed by your request, then please just say that. The second might be intended to convey appreciation for the attention, care, or wisdom you may have received in an interaction. It is so much better to say, "Thank you for listening, or caring, or sharing your wisdom." Thank you for your time is bland and almost insulting. If all you received from the other person was their time, then effectively you received nothing. The time would've passed whether or not this person was in your presence. So if anything of value took place, identify it and be precise in expressing your gratitude.

5. **Hack.** The word *hack* is hackneyed. It is no longer edgy or cool to use this word, which refers to the act of illegally breaking into another person's computer system, as a shortcut for saying *shortcut*.

4. **Everything happens for a reason / If it's meant to be, it's meant to be.** In Muslim cultures people often punctuate any statement about an action or plan for the future with *Inshallah*, meaning "If it be the will of God." "Everything happens for a reason" and "If it's meant to be, it's meant to be" are new age versions of the same sentiment. If you're speaking in a Muslim country and you say *Inshallah* appropriately, or if you are with others who share the metaphysical presuppositions implied in these English phrases, you will connect with the audience, but if your audience isn't Muslim or Aquarian, then abstain.

3. **Woke**, or compounding the lack of originality with profanity for emphasis, **Woke as F**k**. This usage is symptomatic of pretension to the possession of expanded consciousness about social justice. It's misuse of tense is a pandering attempt to seem hip when discussing issues of race, class, gender, and so on.

2. **Badass / superpower.** If you need to read something that says you are one (a badass) or have one (a superpower), then you probably aren't, and you probably don't, respectively. Moreover, badasses don't read self-help books, but many impressive, formidable, and bold individuals do. I grew up on Marvel comics and still enjoy speculating on, and discussing with friends, which superpower would be most fun to have — invisibility, invulnerability, X-ray vision? (I'd actually opt for healing ability.) But selling personal-development courses or self-help books by promoting "superpowers" is destined to be another example of overpromising and underdelivering. Listening, empathy, intuition, creativity, and yes, presentation skills are abilities that we can all cultivate, and they will give

a boost to *our career*, but supercharging is as far as I'm prepared to go. They aren't superpowers.

1. **Whatever.** I confess that I've used this term when I don't feel I have the energy to address the issue that has been raised, or if I think it's not worthy of a more thoughtful response. But since I aspire to be kind to all sentient beings and to improve my language skills, I endeavor to refrain.

Let's give the last word to legendary film producer Samuel Goldwyn, who said, "What we need now is some new, fresh clichés."

Avoid Disclaimer Phrases, a.k.a. Eraser Phrases

Disclaimers, or "eraser phrases," are often weapons of deceit and obfuscation. They're designed to make insults and obnoxious comments more palatable. And unless they're used skillfully for humorous purposes, they're also annoying. Classics include:

> **No offense.** "I'm about to or I have just offended you, and I want to get away with it without consequence or responsibility." Example: "No offense, but I loathe you and think you're an idiot."
>
> **Bless your heart.** A highly nuanced Southern US eraser phrase. ("Can you *believe* that dress she's wearing? Bless her heart.")
>
> **With all due respect.** Often used in the attempt to deny the disrespect intended when insulting someone, particularly a person in a position of authority, like a boss or a judge.
>
> **I don't mean that in a bad way.** The all-purpose eraser phrase popularized by comedian Dom Irrera. Dom explains that in his neighborhood it was commonly

used as follows: "You're a lowlife scummy little fat rat weasel bastard....I don't mean that in a bad way."

Just sayin'. This attempted disclaimer, is number 11 on my list of most annoying phrases. It is similar to "I don't mean that in a bad way" without the wit and is used to avoid taking responsibility for what was just said. "You're a lowlife scummy little fat rat weasel bastard. Just sayin'."

I'm not prejudiced/racist/bigoted/sexist/homophobic, but... A favorite of prejudiced, racist, bigoted, sexist homophobes.

Be that as it may. An old-fashioned way of saying, "Whatever."

I don't mean to interrupt, but... People who say this definitely mean to interrupt, so instead take responsibility and say something like, "Please allow me to interrupt."

Not that there's anything wrong with that. A classic from *Seinfeld*, used to qualify Jerry's denial that he and George are gay.

Use Jargon Only in Context

Do you, like many of my clients, work in an HAC? That's a TLA, Three Letter Acronym, for High Acronym Culture. Jargon, in the form of acronyms, slang, code words, and insider phrases, can be an efficient way to communicate and can help teams build a sense of alignment through a shared language. *But it's useful only if everyone involved understands it.* It is amazing how frequently computer, financial, and automotive salespeople, just to name a few, use jargon that their customers don't understand. In many organizations, the engineers love to use jargon that the marketing department doesn't understand, and marketing gets revenge by making up jargon that *no one* understands. So remember to tune in to your audience and assess how much they understand and appreciate the jargon you use so that you avoid this particular form of, to use a jargon term to which you have been initiated, molecule fondling.

Linguist Tammy Gales explains, "If you do it thoughtfully, then initiating a group into jargon, with careful explanation, can be a powerful tool to engage and bond with them. They feel like 'Hey now I have this new secret language and it is opening a whole new world to me.'"

Eliminate Habitual Interjections

Um, *ah*, *you know*, and *like* are habitual interjections or filler words used unconsciously to begin a sentence, fill a pause, or express a need for confirmation or connection. Overuse of these fillers detracts from your authority and presence. In a recent presentation-skills seminar, the average speaker used sixteen filler words per five-minute video practice session. Professional speakers use none.

Speakers tend to use filler words when they are unprepared or not aligned with their subject. And it's shockingly common even when people are prepared and aligned. The key to eliminating this diminishment of your presence is to practice deleting these interjections in your daily conversation. Be especially vigilant if you are interacting with other people who say "like" and "you know" multiple times in every sentence.

Curse Only Judiciously

"Life," according to legendary free-speech pioneer and comedian Lenny Bruce, "is a four-letter word." Bruce was arrested many times for challenging the restrictions against the use of profanity.

Bruce and others championed our right to curse, but is it wise and effective to swear when you're presenting?

Some argue that cursing demonstrates authenticity. Judging by the profusion of recent bestselling book titles featuring words that in Bruce's era would get you thrown in jail, they may have a point.

Linguist Michael Adams, author of *In Praise of Profanity*, makes the case that in the right circumstances, swearing creates a sense of bonding through a shared experience of rebelling against perceived conventions of "proper" language. The problem comes when this form of rebelling becomes so common that it's no longer the most original way to express yourself.

Comedian and social satirist George Carlin, who was once arrested as an audience member at a Lenny Bruce performance, was gifted in his ability to use what he affectionately termed "dirty words" to get laughs and make people think, but many who have attempted to follow in his footsteps just sound vulgar and aren't particularly funny.

Although in some contexts profanity may help you bond or connect with people, or get a laugh, it also runs the real risk of offending and alienating many others. No professional speaker has ever had a problem because they did not use profanity, so it's probably best to exercise restraint. As Oscar Wilde noted, "There is no mode of action, no form of emotion, that we do not share with the lower animals. It is only by language that we rise above them, or above each other — by language, which is the parent, and not the child, of thought."

Develop Your Vocabulary

Now that you've learned how to eliminate the inessential, let's turn to the second key technique for improving your skill with words: developing your vocabulary.

Renowned as history's greatest genius, Leonardo da Vinci worked earnestly on building his vocabulary throughout his life. The maestro wrote out the definitions of more than nine thousand new words in his famous notebooks.

With an active command of ninety-three thousand words, German polymath and author of *Faust*, Johann Wolfgang von Goethe, had the most expansive vocabulary ever measured. He observed, "The limits of my language are the limits of my universe." If you'd like to expand your universe and your ability to help others expand theirs, which is the broad purpose of public speaking, then expand your vocabulary and your ability to use it precisely. As Steven Pinker explains in *The Language Instinct*, "We can shape events in each other's brains with exquisite precision." But first, of course, we must shape our own cognitive events by expanding our vocabulary and our understanding of the nuances and shades of meaning of the words we use.

The author of the 1916 classic *Thinking as a Science*, Henry Hazlitt, observed, "A man with a scant vocabulary will almost certainly be a weak thinker. The richer and more copious one's vocabulary and the greater one's awareness of fine distinctions and subtle nuances of meaning, the more fertile and precise is likely to be one's thinking. Knowledge of things and knowledge of the words for them grow together. If you do not know the words, you can hardly know the thing."

As you practice inhibiting the use of meaningless phrases, clichés, and filler words, you will be ever more able to fill the void with just the right word at the right time. This strengthens your clarity and your presence and eventually your creativity, too.

In addition to learning new words and using them in your everyday speech, it's helpful to make a practice of looking up the origin of the words you use. If you go to www.etymonline.com, you can instantly get the origin of any word. The word *vocabulary*, for example, is from the medieval Latin *vocabularium*, "a list of words," from the Latin *vocabulum*, "word, name, noun," from *vocare*, "to name, call," related to *vox*, "voice." Expanding your vocabulary and researching word origins will help you discover a voice that is richer, clearer, and more persuasive. A simple way to begin is to subscribe to www.merriam-webster.com/word-of-the-day.

Listen to Great Speakers and Read Great Writers

When I first learned to juggle, I practiced intensively every day and made good progress, but then I joined the International Jugglers' Association (IJA) and started going to open practices with lots of amazing jugglers. I improved rapidly, seemingly through osmosis. I also found that my tennis and chess games improved dramatically when I played with much better players. The same phenomenon takes place when one is surrounded by great speakers and writers, either in real or virtual form.

In the beginning of my speaking career I was fortunate to work with a gifted copresenter — to whom this book is dedicated — and I studied his style and substance diligently. This helped launch my career as a speaker, and I began to be invited to present at global events for many groups, including the Young Presidents' Organization (YPO), featuring many outstanding presenters, and I sought to discover the distinguishing elements of the best of the best.

Today we have TED Talks, Moth Stories, and many other video forums where we can seek to benchmark and model excellence.

Which brings us to our third technique for sharpening our way with words. One of the simplest secrets of becoming a powerful public speaker is to spend as much time as possible listening, watching, and learning from the best. A good place to begin is the list of one hundred great American speeches: www.americanrhetoric.com/top100speechesall.html.

Among my favorites from that list are Martin Luther King Jr. ("I Have a Dream"), Barbara Jordan (keynote speech at the 1976 Democratic Convention), and Ronald Reagan (remarks at Brandenburg Gate). If I could go back in time, I'd aim for a front-row seat at Queen Elizabeth I's speech to her troops at Tilbury, George Washington's farewell remarks, and Lincoln's Gettysburg Address. Of those who are available to be heard, my all-time favorite most powerful public speaker is Winston Churchill. More recently my favorite orators include Alan Watts, Barack Obama (at the 2004 DNC), and Australian prime minster Julia Gillard (her Misogyny Speech in 2012. She really *is* a badass!). And let's add Queen Elizabeth II's elegant address to the British people delivered in the midst of the Covid-19 pandemic. Commentator Greg Hall described it eloquently: "In 523 words — only 248 words more than Abraham Lincoln's Gettysburg Address — the Queen managed to do what no Briton has done in recent memory: unite the country." He continued, "She embodied *ethos*, or character, which the Roman statesman Cicero argued was one of the three qualities that made the best orators, along with *logos* (logic) and *pathos* (emotion)." Like Churchill in his finest hour, the queen used clear, simple language, and her recency effect featured a perfect triad: "We will be with our friends again; we will be with our families again; we will meet again."

Great speakers, and great achievers of all kinds, are inspired by previous greats. Sir Isaac Newton wrote, "I stand on the shoulders of giants." Albert Einstein kept a picture of Newton above his bed. And Einstein continues to inspire physicists and humanists alike. Pioneering educator Maria Montessori was inspired by

Johann Pestalozzi, the man who helped create the school that liberated young Einstein's creative abilities. Michael Jordan modeled his game after David Thompson. LeBron James was inspired by Jordan and now inspires players globally.

Create your own dream team of speakers to inspire you, and complement that team with a crew of writers whose use of language elevates your prose and makes your speech more poetic. The world's first billionaire author and creator of the Harry Potter series, J. K. Rowling explains, "The most important thing is to read as much as you can, like I did. It will give you an understanding of what makes good writing and it will enlarge your vocabulary." J. R. R. Tolkien, author of *The Lord of the Rings*, adds, "A good vocabulary is not acquired by reading books written according to some notion of the vocabulary of one's age group. It comes from reading books above one."

Writers who help me reach above my level include Charles Dickens, Emily Dickinson, Amy Hempel, Hermann Hesse, Wisława Szymborska, Oscar Wilde, and P. G. Wodehouse. And my supreme language paragon of all time is William Shakespeare.

If you want to become a *tower of strength* (*Richard III*) as a public speaker, then *for goodness' sake* (*Henry VIII*) realize that Shakespeare is *the be-all and the end-all* (*Macbeth*), and enjoy this *bedazzling* wisdom for powerful public speaking drawn from his *multitudinous* works:

> **"My words fly up, my thoughts remain below: Words without thoughts never to heaven go."** If you want your presentations to be more heavenly, follow Claudius's advice in *Hamlet*. If you think clearly before you speak and inhibit the use of nonwords, clichés, jargon, curses, and drivel, you'll be more effective.

"Brevity is the soul of wit." Although Polonius doesn't follow the advice he gives to Laertes in *Hamlet*, this line is nevertheless Shakespeare's affirmation of the KISS principle: Keep it simple, speaker. Einstein stated that things "should be made as simple as possible, but no simpler." Seek the optimal simplicity for your expression.

"All the world's a stage." In *As You Like It*, Jaques reminds us that life is theater — and so is every presentation, for better or worse.

And all the men and women merely players;
They have their exits and their entrances,
And one man in his time plays many parts.

In the next chapter we will explore the role of body language in powerful public speaking and, not surprisingly, it is Shakespeare who offers the best counsel on this when in Hamlet's speech to the players he says, "Suit the action to the word, the word to the action."

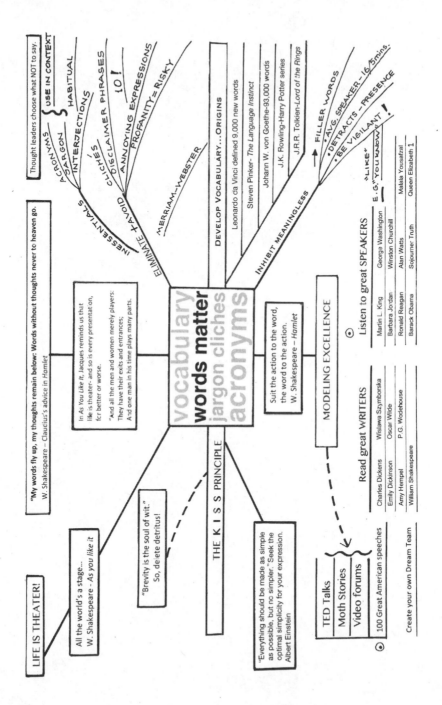

Chapter 7

Cultivate Your Body Language

As you know, verbal language is important. And so is non-verbal language. The big secret is that what really matters is *the alignment and coordination of your verbal and nonverbal communication.* This is what Shakespeare meant when he advised, "Suit the action to the word, the word to the action." When your words say one thing and your body says another, you will feel uncomfortable and anxious, and you will confuse your audience and weaken your credibility, leading to more discomfort and anxiety.

An ancient Chinese proverb states "Beware of the man whose stomach does not move when he laughs." If your stomach doesn't move when you laugh, then your laughter seems phony and forced. Your posture, gestures, and movements can enhance your presentation dramatically, or they can sabotage an otherwise thoughtful and well-organized talk. When your body and your message are in harmony, your audience perceives you as genuine, but if there is a disparity between your words and your posture, gesture, facial expression, or voice tone, they are likely to be suspicious and less receptive.

Your body language will always be more integrated when you have clear objectives for your presentation and a strategy for making it memorable. When people aren't clear about their objectives and haven't organized their message, they say "um" and "ah" more frequently, and they're more likely to have a guarded posture and to make unnecessary gestures and awkward movements. Being well prepared and focused on communicating a message you believe in will do more for your body language than anything else. Preparation and clarity of intention and message are necessary but not always sufficient for great presentations.

Why? Because most people have habits and unconscious patterns of tension that become exaggerated in front of a group, to the detriment of their effectiveness. Professional presenters work on freeing themselves from these constraining habits as they cultivate ever more articulate and powerful body language. I've been studying and teaching methods to cultivate this freedom during my entire career, and in this chapter, I will share with you the most powerful means I've discovered for finding freedom and flow in your presentations and in your life.

Presence: A One-Minute Pose or a Way of Being?

In a study entitled "Power Posing: Brief Nonverbal Displays Affect Neuroendocrine Levels and Risk Tolerance," Amy Cuddy and her colleagues reported on their exploration of this question: "Humans and other animals express power through open, expansive postures, and they express powerlessness through closed, constrictive postures. But can these postures actually cause power?"

Their answer, popularized in Cuddy's TED Talk, is yes.

The researchers concluded, "By simply changing physical posture, an individual prepares his or her mental and physiological systems to endure difficult and stressful situations, and perhaps to actually improve confidence and performance in situations such as interviewing for jobs, speaking in public, disagreeing with a boss." The study also suggests that adopting more powerful body positions may "improve a person's general health and well-being."

Cuddy and her colleagues observed that brief power poses such as imitating the jaunty hands-on-hips stances of Superman or Wonder Woman not only help individuals who adopt them feel more confident, but they also affect the way others perceive those individuals.

In contemporary science this finding has been received as something of a revelation, whereas thespians and martial artists have been studying these effects in a detailed and practical manner for millennia.

You can change your physiology by power posing before presenting, but you'll probably discover that unless you have a practice to make your everyday movements and posture more powerful, the effects of the short-term pose will not be sustainable. And you may look like an idiot.

Body-Message Synchrony:
Aligning Your Body Language with Your Words

In Japan people greet one another with a bow. The traditional salutation in India is the namaste, a slight bow with hands in the prayer position. Hugs and embraces are common in many parts of the world. In many places, the handshake reigns. What do all these gestures have in common? They all convey the reassuring message "I am friend, not foe." Our body language communicates reassurance, authority, confidence, and trustworthiness, or the lack thereof.

People who appear shifty or crooked are viewed with suspicion; those who are straightforward and upright are perceived as honest and strong.

In a study entitled "Attracting Assault: Victims' Nonverbal Cues," Betty Grayson and Morris Stein showed videotapes of people walking down a street in New York City to a group of convicted muggers and asked them to rate each person's "muggability." As you might expect, individuals who displayed an obvious infirmity in their movement were rated most muggable. The muggers also targeted people who moved in a stiff, slumped, awkward, distracted, or aggressive fashion. The least muggable were those with an upright carriage and a relaxed but purposeful gait.

Whenever you enter a meeting room or walk onstage to present, the audience instinctively and immediately assesses your muggability. How can you become less muggable and cultivate a more powerful presence?

Some presentation training courses aim to teach you how to fake authority through power poses, gestures, and dominance cues. It's better to allow your true authority to emerge by cultivating body language that is natural, expressive, and authentic.

You can do this by developing body-message synchrony, ensuring that your posture, movements, gestures, facial expressions, eye contact, voice tone, volume, and inflection are in sync with your message. Start, like professionals do, with authentic passion to communicate something of value to your audience and by clearly defining your objectives and organizing a memorable message. But there's another secret as well: professionals work at unlearning the unnecessary habits that constrain self-expression.

Although the elements of body language function interdependently, let's simplify our approach to unlearning by examining each individually.

Stance

Boxers and martial artists usually adopt some kind of triangular stance so that they offer a minimal target to their opponents. The basic message of a fighter's stance is "You can't hit me and I'm going to hit you." Baseball batters and golfers organize their stance so they can address the ball. Their body language says, "I'm ready to knock this sphere out of the park or onto the green."

As a communicator you usually don't want to give the impression that you're preparing to whack your audience; rather, you want to convey a sense of welcoming, openness, and trust. You do this by facing your audience directly with an upright, balanced, and open stance.

A reliable basic stance is the simplest and most powerful way to cultivate poise and presence, helping you connect with any kind of audience in any circumstance. It also becomes a point of departure for graceful, expressive, confident movement.

The most challenging aspect of an actor's training is not memorizing complex soliloquies or learning strange accents; a would-be thespian's greatest challenge is learning to stand and move in an expansive, natural, unaffected way. Standing in an upright, balanced, and natural way is the most important element in cultivating a commanding stage presence. Here's a wonderful way to cultivate these qualities.

STAND EASE: Don't Just Do Something, Stand There!

Drawn from ancient Chinese lineages, the following practice is the single most effective method I have discovered for developing presence and cultivating life energy. If you practice this a few minutes a day and eventually work your way up to twenty minutes daily, you'll find that you have more energy, confidence, and ease in all your interactions but especially while presenting. Ideally, you would do this in a quiet, beautiful place. I like to practice on a hilltop near my home with a view of the river but also find that it's an ideal activity while waiting at the airport to board a plane, or anywhere else. (You can also apply most of the elements while you're sitting, if you like.)

STAND EASE is an acronym to help you remember the elements that make this simple practice so powerful:

Smile. Begin with a subtle smile, like the Buddha or Mona Lisa. Let the smile shine in your eyes. This shifts your physiology immediately and helps you feel more equanimity. And you'll discover that this genuine smile also helps others feel more relaxed and comfortable in your presence.

Tongue. Gently place the tip of your tongue on your upper palate, just behind your teeth. If you say the phrase *Let go* aloud, you'll notice that as you make the *L* sound in *Let*, your tongue naturally moves to this point. This is an acupuncture point that connects the energy that flows up your back with the energy that flows down your front, thereby helping you feel more balanced and at ease.

Align. Align your body around the vertical axis. That's another way of saying "stand at your full stature." When we're stressed, we tend to contract and diminish our stature, and that compromises our presence and energy. While you practice standing at your full stature, always avoid locking your knees. Keep the knees soft, and remember that they are meant to be weight-transferring joints, not weight-bearing joints.

Natural. If you look at young children or aboriginal people from any culture who haven't been corrupted by so-called civilization, you'll notice that they are up-right and aligned around the vertical axis in a natural, easy way. Sitting in chairs all day makes it easy to forget that this natural poise is your birthright.

Distribute. With your feet about shoulder-width apart, sense the feeling of your feet on the floor. Distribute your weight evenly between your feet, and between the ball, heel, and inner and outer parts of each foot. Even weight distribution gives a message of evenness and balance to your whole nervous system and supports psychophysical equilibrium.

Exhale. Exhalation encourages relaxation and stress release. Exhale by compressing your belly, lower ribs, and lower back. When under stress, people tend to gasp for air and try too hard to breathe in, over-activating the upper chest and neck muscles. Instead, breathe out from your center, and then just allow the air in through your nose gently. Breathing easily, slowly, and smoothly from your center will help you feel more centered.

Aware. Awaken and expand your awareness. Attune to everything within and around you. When we are overstressed, we tend to narrow our focus. By expanding our attention we also expand our sense of ease and the power of our presence.

Soften. Soften your eyes and your belly. Feel the weight of your shoulders and your jaw, and you'll notice that they soften, too. Maintain your alignment, and let everything be soft.

Expand. Allow your energy and presence to expand. (As you practice STAND EASE over time, you may begin to notice an effortless and enjoyable sense of buoyancy and energetic expansion.) When you're preparing to present, intentionally fill the entire room with your energy and presence. Create a welcoming field of vivacity. Don't be surprised when people come up to you after you present and say something like, "Wow! I feel so energized by your presentation!"

In addition to daily formal practice of this standing meditation, you can also practice the stance in everyday life. Instead of fidgeting or checking a device when you're waiting in line, you can practice STAND EASE. As you practice over the weeks and months, you'll begin to discover that you feel more at home and comfortable in your body and that you can transfer that poise to social situations and ultimately to developing a powerful presence onstage.

In other words, *Don't just do something, stand there!* As the Tao Te Ching advises, "In stillness the muddied water returns to clarity." If you want to be clear and present, then practice this simple standing meditation.

Movement

The stillness you cultivate through standing meditation sets the stage for developing more grace and power in all your movements, both in everyday life and on the stage. The human brain is designed to follow movement. And when you're presenting, you're communicating with your audience through every movement, consciously or not. When your movements are in sync with the flow of communication, they add depth and resonance to your message. When they're out of sync, they may sabotage your communication. For example, rocking and swaying movements might be fine if you are speaking about drunkenness or the perils of ocean travel and using these movements for illustrative purposes. But if you are just shifting around unconsciously, you may distract or even nauseate your audience.

You can discover and begin to unlearn your unnecessary, unconscious movements by watching yourself on video, ideally with the help of a supportive and perspicacious friend or colleague who will give you accurate feedback. While learning to let go of distracting movements, avoid the trap of standing frozen in place. If you are not confident in your movement, invest more time exploring the basic stance.

When you free yourself from unconscious, habitual distracting movements, you'll discover that natural, expressive movements emerge effortlessly, like, for example, walking toward the audience to emphasize a particularly important point or moving from one side of the room, stage, or riser to the other to emphasize your connection with the whole audience.

Gestures

Many years ago, some friends and I spent a summer traveling through Italy. We arrived in Rome with a list of three recommended pensioni, inexpensive bed-and-breakfasts. The first place on our list, Pensione Rosa, had no vacancies. The second, Pensione Alberto, was also full. We asked the owner if he could tell us if we were likely to find room at Pensione Anna, the last place on our list.

Alberto responded by repeating the name Pensione Anna as he drew his sleeve, all the way from his shoulder to his fingertips, across his nose. He completed this gesture of unqualified disgust by casting a large quantity of imaginary nasal discharge violently to the floor. His gesture was so powerful that decades later if a friend mentions traveling to Rome, I'm quick to warn, "Don't stay at Pensione Anna!"

Gestures have tremendous impact on your effectiveness as a communicator. There are two keys to making that impact positive. The first is to avoid unnecessary gestures. Change rattling, pen fondling, excessive face scratching, nose wiping, hair adjusting, and genital guarding are among the most common nervous gestures that create unintended results. Observe yourself in a mirror or on video, and pare superfluous gestures from your presentation. If you aren't sure what to do with your hands, just allow them to rest at your sides.

The second key is to discover your natural gestural language and exaggerate it. Although you do not have to go as far as Alberto, you can increase your impact by telling your story with your hands. Let your natural gestural language emerge and expand. Just as you need to increase the projection of your voice to reach a large group, you must project your gestures.

Shyness leads many people to suppress their natural gestural expression. With appropriate feedback, however, you can overcome this self-limitation.

An executive of a Swedish shipping company provides a delightful example. In a presentation meant to describe his company's most impressive vessel, he held his hands in front of his solar plexus no more than a few inches apart. As he watched himself on video, he realized that this was not an accurate gestural representation of his company's flagship. His smile suggested that he understood the need to move beyond his self-imposed constraint.

In the next take, he doubled the size of his gesture. But the video clearly demonstrated that his gestural frame was still too small for the picture he intended to convey. Mustering his courage for a final take, he flung his arms to full horizontal extension while booming out the words, "We have really big tanker."

Later, when he watched the tape, he was amazed to discover that the gesture, which had felt grossly exaggerated to him, actually looked natural and appropriately expressive.

You can awaken your natural expression by watching yourself on video. Study how your exaggerated gestures complement your message. Other useful exercises include miming your presentation, experimenting with gestures in everyday conversation, and playing charades.

Shakespeare provided the essential wisdom on gesture and body-message synchrony in *Hamlet*, when he reminded us: "Suit the action to the word, the word to the action." For most people this means being *more expressive* by making bigger more dramatic gestures. Shakespeare counseled, "Be not too tame."

Of course, some folks get carried away and overdo it, and that can distract from the power of your presence. Shakespeare warned, "Do not saw the air too much with your hand, thus." He guides us to discover poise — the right amount of energy in the right place at the right time — by expressing ourselves powerfully and gracefully, advising, "for in the very torrent, tempest, and, as I may say, the whirlwind of passion, you must acquire and beget a temperance that may give it smoothness." And, ultimately you discover this for yourself through your own exploration and self-reflection. In Shakespeare's words, "let your own discretion be your tutor."

Eye Contact

Boxers, mixed martial artists, and other fighters aim to gain an advantage before the contest begins by establishing dominant eye contact. The eyeballing between Muhammad Ali and Joe Frazier in the Thrilla in Manila match, and the gaze between Wanderlei Silva and Mirko Cro Cop in their first UFC battle, are among the most chilling examples. As one comment on the latter encounter expressed it, "Silva looks like he's about to kill someone. Cro Cop looks like he already has." (You can see original footage if you do an internet search for "best staredowns in fighting history.")

On a much gentler and more romantic note, at the end of the Academy Award–winning film *Casablanca*, Ingrid Bergman and Humphrey Bogart communicate volumes of heart-wrenching emotion through what is perhaps the greatest eye-contact scene in movie history, rivaled only by the phenomenal ocularly mediated magic between Leonardo DiCaprio and Claire Danes in Baz Luhrmann's 1996 version of Shakespeare's *Romeo and Juliet*. Their portrayal of love at first sight, as their eyes meet across a fish tank, offers a defining image for that classic phrase.

Our eyes, as Shakespeare observed, are "the windows of the soul." They express the full range of human experience, from threat and terror to intimacy and passion. Of course, in most presentations you are not trying to stare down or romance your audience. Your aim is to make contact so you can keep their interest and communicate your message. Eye contact enables you to read your audience and monitor your effectiveness. Is your audience bored? Are they confused? Enraptured? Tired? The answer is right in front of your eyes.

When you're making a point in a conversation with a friend, you naturally watch your friend's eyes to monitor the state of connection and to see if she's understood what you're saying. If her expression appears quizzical, you may ask if she has a question about what you're saying. If your eyes wander off while your friend is speaking to you, she might ask you to return your focus to her.

Eye contact is normal and natural in everyday conversation, and professionals know that it is as well when speaking to a group. Making eye contact with members of your audience promotes a sense of connectedness and rapport that makes them much more available to your influence.

When you engage people's eyes, you establish trust, draw interest, and access channels of influence. Although relatively easy in one-to-one communication, many speakers find it difficult to make eye contact with people in groups. This difficulty usually stems from viewing the audience as an impersonal mass. However large your audience, you can still speak to them as individuals.

If you are uncomfortable making eye contact with an audience, try this exercise. While you're standing onstage or at the front of a meeting room, pick out the friendliest-looking people sitting to your right, your left, and straight in front. Use them as anchors for eye contact. Engage their eyes for two or three seconds at a time. By focusing on representatives from each part of the room, you give the whole audience a greater sense of your involvement and interest in them. As you become comfortable with your friendly anchors, expand your gaze to meet other members of the audience.

When you master this, try a more challenging exercise. Seek out the unfriendliest-looking people from each part of the room, and draw them out by engaging their eyes in a confident and friendly manner.

I once attempted this while giving an after-dinner speech to a group of investment bankers. The group was just finishing an elaborate meal that had begun with cocktails and proceeded through several wine-accompanied courses. As they sniffed their cognac and settled back in their chairs, I rose to deliver my remarks.

Among the many tired and distracted candidates for anchors, I chose three granite-faced bankers who seemed committed to acting as though there was no speaker. Launching into the presentation, I sought them out with my eyes, looking beyond their apparent disinterest. Halfway through the speech, two of the three shifted their positions. Their postures opened and their eyes said they were with me. The third fellow remained slumped over, arms tightly folded, expressionless.

As I began my closing, I could see from the nods and thoughtful looks that the audience, with the exception of my third anchor, was getting the message. I made one last attempt to draw him out with my eyes, to no avail. Finally, I spoke my last sentence — just as he passed out and collapsed on the floor!

I can't guarantee 100 percent success — or that you'll win over two out of three hostile listeners and knock the third one out cold. But you will find that natural, lively eye contact is fundamental to mastering the art of public speaking.

And you'll prepare yourself for success in front of a group if you practice seeing with alert, receptive "listening" eyes in your everyday conversations.

Voice

When I was in junior high I'd stay awake for hours after bedtime contemplating the meaning of life and the vast emptiness of the cosmos. Why were we created? What if we didn't exist? What happens when we die? These questions made me anxious, and to help me fall asleep I relied on a golden globe-shaped radio that I kept tuned to a station that featured what former FBI hostage negotiator and founder of the Black Swan Group Chris Voss calls "a late-night FM DJ voice." When I remember the sound of that voice from decades ago I feel more relaxed in the present. Voss trains his students to use that voice to help put others at ease in stressful negotiations, and he emphasizes the importance of shifting one's tone of voice as a means of directly influencing the brain, mood, and attitude of one's counterparts.

Your voice has a profound effect on your communication, whether in a negotiation or a presentation. Try a little experiment. Pick any sentence or phrase and alter its meaning by changing your tone, inflection, and volume. For example, try to make the words "Yes, I am sure you are right" mean "No, I am sure you are wrong."

In addition to inverting the meaning of words, your voice can express an amazing range of complexities and nuances of meaning. Consider, for example, how much you may know from the tone of voice with which a friend or relative answers the telephone. Can you sometimes tell that someone is depressed or annoyed or excited and enthusiastic just from the way they say "hello"?

The tone, inflection, pacing, and volume of your voice have a powerful effect on others in all aspects of life and especially in public speaking. And in virtual presentations, your voice becomes even more important.

Let's consider how you can use your voice to accomplish your objectives.

Expressive Variation

Do you know why you are able to fall asleep despite the rumblings of your air conditioner or the sounds of traffic passing outside the window? Your brain contains a marvelous system called the reticular activating mechanism. It tunes out repetitive noise. The same mechanism wakes you in response to a sound that stands out from a monotonous background, such as your alarm ringing.

Unfortunately for boring speakers, the reticular activating mechanism also helps an audience sleep through presentations delivered in a monotone voice. By varying your tone, inflection, and volume in coordination with your content, you send a stream of wake-up calls to your audience's brains, dramatically increasing the impact and memorability of your presentation. So, for example, when you lower your volume and slow your pace, you can create anticipation for what you're about to say. When you ask a question, what would it sound like if you used a questioning tone of voice? When you want to express passion, you might raise your volume. But if you do any of these exclusively, audiences will tune you out just like a rumbling air conditioner. So mix it up!

The Power of the Pause

Um, ah, the pause is, you know, uh, like, a really important part of, ah, using the, ah, voice. The average speaker is afraid to pause. As a result, most people either talk too fast or use filler noises such as *um, ah, you know,* and *like.*

In the Tao Te Ching, Chinese sage Lao Tzu reflected,

We join spokes together in a wheel,
but it is the center hole
that makes the wagon move.

We shape clay into a pot,
but it is the emptiness inside
that holds whatever we want.

We hammer wood for a house,
but it is the inner space
that makes it livable.

We work with being,
but non-being is what we use.

The pause is the hub, the hollow, that brings your words to life. Pausing gives you time to breathe, to center yourself, to think. It gives your audience the opportunity to absorb and reflect on your message. Pausing conveys confidence as it captivates your audience's attention.

Develop your "pauseability" by recording and listening to yourself. Experiment with extending your pauses. Explore appropriate timing. Notice the frequency of filler words, and strive to eliminate them. Instead of *um*-ing and *ah*-ing, pause. Pausing at the right time has a hypnotic effect on an audience. It draws them to you. And it allows you to breathe fully and think about what you're saying.

As Mark Twain observed, "The right word may be effective, but no word was ever as effective as a rightly timed pause." Twain pays tribute to the power of the pause in poetic terms: "That impressive silence, that eloquent silence, that geometrically progressive silence which often achieves a desired effect where no combination of words howsoever felicitous could accomplish it."

And he explains how he developed his attunement to the timing of the pause: "For one audience, the pause will be short; for another a little longer; for another a shade longer still; the performer must vary the length of the pause to suit the shades of difference between audiences....I used to play with the pause as other children play with a toy."

I was thrilled when I discovered these reflections from Twain because they mirror my own learning and method; playing with the pause like a toy and reading the audience's response in the moment is a delicious expression of mastery to which we can all aspire. Learning to pause appropriately onstage, online, or in front of a conference room is a simple, powerful way to establish authority and demonstrate confidence. If you want to do this with confidence when presenting, you must practice in your everyday conversations.

Integrating Stance, Movement, Gesture, Eyes, and Voice with the Alexander Technique

Your voice rides on your breath. Free breathing liberates your voice, and a balanced, expansive upright posture frees your breathing. As you develop your basic stance and ease of movement, your breathing and voice will improve. And, as noted above, pausing gives you time to breathe and make eye contact with your audience. Moreover, your brain is about 3 percent of your body's weight, but it uses about 30 percent of your oxygen intake, so fuller, easier breathing means a more oxygenated brain, which leads to greater clarity and presence while speaking.

Despite a sometimes grueling speaking schedule, I have never lost my voice. I apply a method that gives me access to the natural, expressive, and authentic use of my voice and body language. This same method is also an effective means for developing self-knowledge, changing habits, and transforming fear. It is called the Alexander Technique, named after its founder, F.M. Alexander. Alexander Technique teachers use their hands in an exquisitely subtle manner to give their students an experience of ease of movement and freedom from the unconscious and unnecessary tension that interferes with breathing, vocal usage, and stage presence. Frank Jones, former director of the Tufts University Institute for Psychological Research, describes the technique as "a means for changing stereotyped response patterns by the inhibition of certain postural sets" and as "a method for expanding consciousness to take in inhibition as well as excitation (i.e., 'not doing' as well as 'doing') and thus obtaining a better integration of the reflex and voluntary elements in a response pattern."

My favorite description of the technique was offered by

Gertrude Stein's brother Leo, who called it "the method for keeping your eye on the ball applied to life."

The technique is taught at the world's premiere theater and music schools, such as the Juilliard School and the Royal Academy of Dramatic Art. It's a trade secret of many of the world's great performing artists, including Paul Newman, Joanne Woodward, Sting, John Cleese, Mary Steenburgen, Sir Georg Solti, Sir Paul McCartney, Deborah Domanski, John Houseman, Jennifer Jason Leigh, Hal Holbrook, Sigourney Weaver, David Hyde Pierce, Bernadette Peters, and Sir Ian McKellen.

When I began my speaking career, I was usually the youngest person in the room. The Alexander Technique gave me a sense of poise and presence that allowed me to hold my ground in interactions with people senior to me. Now I'm often the oldest person in the room, but I usually have the most energy and the best posture, thanks to this technique.

In addition to daily practice of STAND EASE you can also cultivate a stronger, clearer presence by studying the Alexander Technique. Ideally, you would take private lessons with a qualified teacher and/or attend a workshop, but in the meantime, here is a simple practice that can help you get started.

The Balanced Resting State

All you need to benefit from this procedure is a relatively quiet place, some carpeted floor space, a few paperback books, and fifteen to twenty minutes.

Begin by placing the books on the floor. Stand approximately your body's length away from the books, with your feet shoulder-width apart. Let your hands rest gently at your sides. Facing away from the books, look straight ahead with a soft, alert focus. Pause for a few moments. Review the elements of STAND EASE.

Breathing freely, become aware of your feet on the floor, and notice the distance from your feet to the top of your head. Keep your eyes open and alive, and listen to the sounds around you for a few moments.

Then, moving lightly and easily, ease yourself down to the floor. Supporting yourself with your hands behind you, place your feet on the floor in front of you, with knees bent. Continue breathing easily.

Let your head drop forward a bit to ensure that you are not tightening your neck muscles and pulling your head back. Then, gently roll your spine along the floor so that your head rests on the books. The books should be positioned so that they support your head at the place where your neck ends and your head begins. If your head is not well positioned, reach back with one hand and support your head while using the other hand to place the books in the proper position. Add or take away books until you find a height that encourages a gentle lengthening of your neck muscles. Your feet remain flat on the floor, with your knees pointing up to the ceiling and your hands resting on the floor or loosely folded on your chest. Allow the weight of your body to be fully supported by the floor.

Rest in this position. As you rest, gravity will lengthen your spine and realign your torso. Keep your eyes open to avoid dozing off. Bring your attention to the flow of your breathing and to the gentle pulsation of your whole body. Be aware of the ground supporting your back, allowing your shoulders to rest as your back widens. Let your neck be free as your whole body lengthens and expands.

After you have rested for fifteen to twenty minutes, get up slowly, being careful to avoid stiffening or shortening your body as you return to a standing position. To achieve a smooth transition, decide when you are going to move, and then gently roll over onto your front, maintaining your new sense of integration and expansion. Ease your way into a crawling position, and then up onto one knee. With your head leading the movement upward, stand up.

Pause for a few moments. Listen. Again, feel your feet on the floor and notice the distance between your feet and the top of your head. You may be surprised to discover that the distance has expanded. Review STAND EASE. As you move into the activities of your day, avoid compromising this expansion, ease, and overall uplift. In other words, be mindful, and free yourself from the habits of hunching over your steering wheel while driving, clasping your toothbrush with a death grip, craning your neck and narrowing your shoulders to manipulate your cell phone, or raising your shoulders to slice a carrot in the kitchen. As you cultivate more mindful and graceful movement in daily life, you'll discover that doing so supports a much greater sense of ease and poise when you're in front of a group to present.

For best results, make the Balanced Resting State a daily practice. You can do it when you wake up in the morning, when you come home from work, or before retiring at night. If you don't have fifteen to twenty minutes, you can still benefit by investing five to ten minutes. The procedure is especially valuable when you are preparing to give a presentation, since it effortlessly helps you manifest an upright, easy poise.

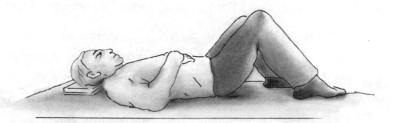

The Balanced Resting State

In her critically acclaimed 2008 debut with the Santa Fe Opera, in the role of Princess Zenobia in Handel's *Radamisto*, lyric mezzo-soprano Deborah Domanski began one of her arias while rolling along the stage floor after being launched from an unfurling carpet. When asked how she was able to project her voice so that it could be enjoyed in the back rows of the packed 2,200-seat outdoor theater, Domanski explained, "My daily practice of the Balanced Resting State and lessons with my Alexander Technique teachers make all the difference." Twelve years later Domanski sings with even richer tone and more multidimensional coloratura, all with less effort and greater stage presence. Her secret? "My voice teacher, the legendary actress and vocalist Beret Arcaya, is also an amazing Alexander Technique teacher. She's thirty years older than me, and she sings beautifully. She's taught me how to access ever greater freedom of movement and breath and the result is that singing gets easier and my voice is more reliable." Domanski, who also teaches voice and stage presence to professional singers and public speakers, adds, "When people stop trying too hard and learn to allow the voice to float on the breath like a surfer rides a wave or an eagle rides a thermal, they're often amazed at the quality of the sound that emerges."

DOSE: The Easy-to-Prepare Elixir to Transform Fear

Balanced Resting State and the STAND EASE meditation, practiced daily, are two of the simplest and most effective means for strengthening your presence through upright, aligned body language. And if you study the Alexander Technique, you'll be tuning your public speaking instrument like Yo-Yo Ma tunes his cello.

Nevertheless, despite everything you've practiced, acute fear can still arise as you anticipate giving a presentation, and I want you to be prepared with a few more simple, practical methods for overcoming it. Fear releases powerful hormones into your bloodstream, with corresponding muscular contractions. This reaction, called the fight-or-flight response, is instinctive. Nature designed it to mobilize us to escape from, or fight with, would-be predators.

Before or during speaking engagements, however, it's not good form to dash out of the room or to physically assault the audience. So most speakers just sit there, tightening up and stewing in their own stress juices as they wait their turn. I call this sitting in the CAN, an acronym that stands for cortisol, adrenaline, and norepinephrine. These are the stress biochemicals that are streaming through your system when you experience stage fright.

DOSE is an acronym for the biochemicals that you can access to get those butterflies into formation: dopamine, oxytocin, serotonin, and endorphins, which are sometimes known as the "happiness chemicals" or the "angel's cocktail."

How can you get out of the CAN? Give yourself a DOSE! Here are a few ways to do that.

Work Out

The simplest and most effective thing you can do to adjust your physiology is to work out before you present. If possible, arrange to do vigorous exercise earlier in the day when you are scheduled to speak. You'll get the most benefit from an intense activity that makes you pour sweat. Hitting a heavy bag or whacking a racquetball or pickleball are ideal movements. By acting out the activities of running and hitting, you release the dammed-up energies of fight-or-flight and shift into flow.

If you can't make it to the gym, then instead of basting in anxiety, find a private space and do some of the following pre-presentation warm-ups. You will metabolically transform your stress juices into happiness chemicals and begin to release the corresponding patterns of muscular contraction.

Shadowbox

If you can't run, hit a heavy bag, or pound a ball against the wall, try shadowboxing. Dance around and throw some punches for three minutes. You'll be surprised at how much better you feel.

Make Funny Faces and Laugh Loudly

Fear can lead you to take your presentation, and yourself, far too seriously, leading you to freeze your face into a rigid, zombie-like mask. Do what professional actors do, and save face by making funny faces. Stand in front of a mirror and make the most fearful look you can muster. Experiment with a full range of extreme expressions. Try anger, surprise, sadness, and joy. Finish by making the stupidest faces imaginable. Let your jaw slacken as your tongue hangs out. Then deliver the first few minutes of your presentation in this slack-jawed silly manner. Besides encouraging a more lighthearted attitude, these exercises mobilize your face and make you look and feel more relaxed and expressive. If you practice looking like an idiot before you present, you're less likely to look like one while you speak.

Making funny faces is also a reliable way to make yourself laugh, and laughter is one of the best ways to stimulate endorphin production and transmute stress.

Listen to Your Favorite Uplifting Music

On his way to the arena, and in the locker room before the game, LeBron James, and many of his colleagues, enjoy their favorite tunes on headphones. High-performing athletes in every sport know that the right music helps gear them up to perform at their best. The same thing is true for public speaking. A study recently published in *Proceedings of the National Academy of Sciences* explains what James and his colleagues know through experience: listening to the music you love will make your brain release more dopamine.

Enjoy Some Aromatherapy and Chocolateopathy

The scents of lavender and vanilla stimulate the production of endorphins, and so does dark chocolate. Dark chocolate is a great "pregame snack" for presenters, and a whiff of lavender or vanilla is a proven mood booster. You can even find dark chocolate infused with lavender and vanilla. Have a little before you speak, and then plan to have more when you're done as a celebration. Anticipating celebration raises dopamine levels significantly.

Connect with the Audience Informally

As we learned in an earlier chapter, arriving early for your presentation allows you to meet members of your audience. Besides the benefit you get from discovering what may be on their minds, you'll also find that if you can connect with a few people, making genuine eye contact, exchanging smiles, handshakes, and ideally hugs, you feel *so much more relaxed and connected* with the audience before you begin. The interpersonal connection releases oxytocin and helps you and the audience feel more at ease.

As you get out of the CAN and give yourself a DOSE in the manner prescribed above, you'll find yourself using much more natural, poised, and expressive body language.

Eva Selhub, former clinical director of the Benson-Henry

Center for Mind Body Medicine and a leading expert on stress and resilience, comments, "These simple practices can help you gain control of your own biochemistry so you can access a sense of well-being, and a more open state of mind, that will translate into more ease and clarity during a public presentation. The stress hormones and stress systems that are normally overactivated when an individual feels threatened or disconnected are kept in check, therefore inhibiting the detrimental and harmful effects of stress and the associated by-products, thus allowing for more social connection and attraction."

She adds, "My endorsement of these practices is more than just my opinion as a scientific researcher; it's also based on my experience as a professional public speaker myself."

Here is one more practice to help you be at your best when you speak publicly.

Getting the Stress Out of Your Bones

In a recent study published in the journal *Cell Metabolism*, Gerard Karsenty and his colleagues share their research into the role of our bones in the stress response. Karsenty explains that our bones release the hormone osteocalcin in response to acute stress. The study included measuring osteocalcin levels in subjects who were experiencing stage fright.

Standing meditation aligns and strengthens the bones, and that may be part of why it's so effective in generating an abiding sense of calm. A complementary practice evolved over thousands of years is particularly useful in preventing or reversing the fight-or-flight response. It's called Bone Marrow Cleansing. Here's the simplest version that can help you get the stress out of your bones just before you go onstage.

Adopt your best standing posture, and apply STAND EASE

for thirty seconds. Begin by gently shaking your whole body, bouncing up and down while keeping your feet on the floor. Kindergarten teachers call this "getting your wiggles out," and it happens to be an ancient energy-harmonizing practice that is also ideal for grown-ups. You get the most benefit, however, if you do it as a child would, with abandon. What are you abandoning? Overseriousness, anxiety, and osteocalcin! Bounce and shake for about a minute, and in the last twenty seconds go all out and add some sighing and blithering sounds for maximum benefit. Then come to complete stillness. Do STAND EASE for thirty seconds. You'll feel your hands and much of the rest of your body tingling in a pleasurable way.

Next, as you inhale through your nose, reach out and up toward the sky with palms up. Look up to the sky, and form the intention of gathering the creative, healing energy of the universe. As you draw the breath in, your lower belly expands. Then as you begin to exhale through either nose or mouth, you look within as your palms turn to face the Earth, with the intention of washing your whole being, right through to your bone marrow, with the creative, healing energy you just gathered. Wash through your whole body, and release any remaining stress, tension, and osteocalcin into the Earth. Repeat for seven cycles.

All these practices will help you get out of the CAN and give you a DOSE. To get the most benefit, and to prepare yourself for long-term success in mastering the art of public speaking, maintain a daily practice that promotes the integration of body, mind, and heart. In this chapter I've shared with you much of what I've learned and what I myself practice. In addition to working out, listening to beautiful music, and enjoying dark chocolate, I do the STAND EASE meditation and apply the Alexander Technique and the Balanced Resting State *every day* so that when I present it's easy to feel poised and present.

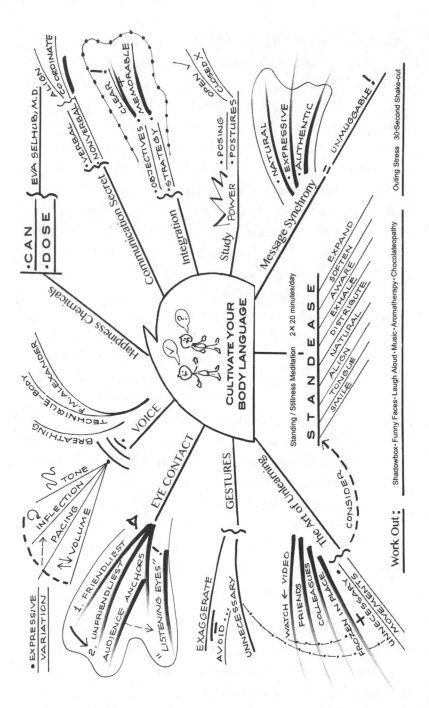

Chapter 8

If the Buddha
Gave Sales Presentations

"He was trying to sell me a bill of goods."

That's the phrase my Grandpa Jack used to indicate that someone was attempting to swindle him. A Ukrainian Jewish immigrant, Jack was a self-made man who worked his way up from sewing in a sweatshop to running his own dress business. He understood that his customers, women doing housework, wanted to wear something beautiful. So with impeccable logic he asked, "Who are the best designers?" The answer was obvious to him: "The Italians."

Jack hired Rosa, an Italian American painter and designer who had just returned from an art tour of Paris. It was love at first sight, and he proposed to her on her first day on the job. She was hesitant, but Jack persevered and eventually sold her on the idea. Besides owing my existence to Jack's sales abilities, I'm also indebted to him because he was a wonderful role model in many ways.

Besides his hard work, creativity, and keen sense of quality and value, he had the characteristic shared by the most wonderful leaders, what Rudyard Kipling called "the common touch." Jack treated all his stakeholders with respect and fairness and was especially generous with his long-term employees, for whom he instituted one of the first profit-sharing programs in the garment district of the Lower East Side of New York City.

The world has changed significantly since Grandpa Jack's time, although the importance of values like hard work, creativity, quality, value, respect, and fairness continues.

In some ways it's harder to be sold a bill of goods today because of the accessibility of information. It's only recently that we have been able to go online and research the actual price of an automobile, for example, so we are not in the dark when we negotiate with a salesperson. And thanks to Yelp, Tripadvisor, and other similar sites, we can read reviews of almost everything.

Yet, as technology evolves, so do the schemes of high-pressure salespeople and con artists. As the Better Business Bureau advises, "Sales scams are as old as humanity, but the Internet has introduced a whole new way to rip people off. For 100 years, BBB has been advising consumers: If it sounds too good to be true, it probably is. That hasn't changed just because the scam artist is coming into your home through your computer or telephone instead of the front door."

Scammers and con artists are more prevalent and virulent than ever. And there's a reason they're called "artists." If you read *Catch Me If You Can*, the book based on Frank W. Abagnale's early life as a forger and an imposter, or watched the movie starring Leonardo DiCaprio, you'll marvel at the protagonist's skill at connecting with others and understanding their needs and desires. Skills that the real Frank now uses as one of the world's most respected authorities on forgery and fraud prevention, as a consultant to the FBI, and as a highly successful professional speaker.

What transformed Frank from a criminal purveyor of fraud into a crusader for its prevention? He says it wasn't prison or religion but, rather, love. Frank explains that meeting his wife (they've now been married thirty-six years and have three children) changed his life, saying, "I was lucky enough to find someone who believed in me."

So what's the difference between selling ideas through the art of the con and through the art of connection?

Intention.

In Hollywood, and in Washington, DC, they say, "Sincerity is the key to success and once you can fake that you've got it made." Actors earn their living by faking sincerity, and so do most politicians.

One of the secrets of success and happiness, outside Hollywood and DC, is finding what you sincerely believe will make the world a better place and selling that. This principle applies to the 10 percent of folks who earn their living directly from sales and to the other 90 percent of us who are engaged every day in attempting to get others to buy in to our ideas.

Two Questions to Change the World

Cynics believe that "nice guys finish last," but they forget that "the winner of the rat race is still a rat." Cynics say, "He who has the gold rules," but the happiest people really do live by the Golden Rule. About forty years ago I had an experience right out of a *New Yorker* cartoon that emphasized this point. As an enthusiastic seeker of spiritual truth, I received word that a renowned meditation master was coming to town to teach. Although the event was not publicized, I managed to discover the time and place and traveled to an obscure location. The room was overflowing with aspirants, and the air was charged with expectation.

After a preparatory period of prayer and meditation, the master appeared. I was on the edge of my prayer cushion, waiting for pearls of esoteric insight, when he proclaimed, "Don't do bad, do good." He then bowed and left.

Before you sell anything — anything! — consider your intention. Don't do bad, do good! Aligning our intentions with fundamental goodness is the key to happiness, for ourselves and others. The insights and methods of sales, influence, and persuasion that we will explore are powerful and must be used only for good.

Keeping this in mind is essential, whether you're in a professional sales job where your livelihood depends on people buying your product or service or you're in a personal interaction where you're aiming to, for example, persuade your partner to move to a new location or get your son to sign up for Mandarin lessons.

"Be sure," as Daniel Pink, author of *To Sell Is Human: The Surprising Truth about Moving Others*, recommends, that "you can answer the two questions.... If the person you're selling to agrees to buy, will his or her life improve? When your interaction is over, will the world be a better place than when you began?" With these two questions you can change the world, by aligning your actions with basic goodness. Many people sell products or services that don't meet these ethical criteria because they just don't know any better.

Steve Lishansky, author of *The Ultimate Sales Revolution: Sell Differently. Change the World*, explains, "Sales must be the ultimate ethical and effective practice of communication, relationship building, influence, and ultimately the maximization of value creation." He adds, "Done this way, it becomes a universal practice of maximizing the contribution and value you can provide another person."

The phrase *caveat emptor* means "let the buyer beware," and there's good reason for this caution. Old-paradigm selling remains associated with, as Grandpa Jack would say, "a bill of goods." A particular body spray will not make you a babe or dude magnet, and a highly caffeinated sugary drink won't give you wings, but it may cause diabetes. Wearing a particular brand of shoes will not make you a better athlete, and drinking a particular brand of beer will not make you more interesting.

Many products, services, and political candidacies are sold through false promises, as this adaptation of an ancient joke illuminates. Joe, a salesman, has a heart attack and dies unexpectedly. He finds himself in the lobby of heaven, where he's greeted by St. Peter. St. Peter explains that the afterlife is a matter of choice and offers him the opportunity to tour heaven and hell before deciding where to spend eternity.

Peter takes Joe by the hand for a quick tour of heaven. It is a tranquil place with lovely harp music and soothing golden light, populated by serene souls who are floating in a meditative state on billowy clouds.

Joe thinks it's nice, but then he takes the elevator down to hell, where he's greeted personally by Satan, who bears an uncanny resemblance to the "Most Interesting Man in the World."

Satan guides Joe through a large golden door to a rollicking scene — rock bands are playing, Harleys are revving, beautiful women wearing bikinis and white go-go boots are spinning around silver poles, and taps are flowing freely with top-shelf alcohol.

After a tantalizing glimpse, Satan escorts Joe to the elevator and he's whisked back to the lobby, where St. Peter asks Joe for his decision. Somewhat embarrassed, Joe tells Peter that heaven was pleasant but hell was what he'd always dreamed of. Peter puts Joe on the one-way elevator back to hell.

When Joe arrives he is horrified to see that the bands, drinks, and Harleys are gone, and so are the dancing girls. Instead there's nothing except an endless display of televisions, and on every channel there's the same pitchman trying to sell something that no one really needs.

Joe finds the Devil and asks, "What the hell is going on? When you gave me a tour it was the party of a lifetime, and now there's nothing but this stupid TV infomercial."

"Ahh, it's simple," replies Satan. "During the tour you were a prospect and now you're a client!"

Don't be like Satan. Always be impeccable with your word, and manage expectations by promising low and delivering high.

Before we begin to explore the most effective and ethical ways to generate buy-in to ideas, let's consider two basic assumptions:

1.   We are all in sales.
2.   Effective selling is based on skills that everyone can learn.

We Are All in Sales

We are all in sales, and selling is part of everyday life. As legendary motivational speaker Zig Ziglar commented, "Maybe you don't hold the title of salesperson, but if the business you are in requires you to deal with people, you, my friend, are in sales."

Grandpa Jack had to sell Grandma Rosa on the idea of marrying him. If you have kids, you need to sell them on the importance of doing their homework. If you have a creative idea, then you must enroll others to make it a reality. Everyone, from artists to zoologists, is engaged in selling ideas, personally and professionally.

Dan Pink makes a powerful case that sales skills are critical to our success, whatever we do: "Physicians sell patients on a remedy. Lawyers sell juries on a verdict. Teachers sell students on the value of paying attention in class. Entrepreneurs woo funders, writers sweet-talk producers, coaches cajole players. Whatever our profession, we deliver presentations to fellow employees and make pitches to new clients."

The Oxford English Dictionary (*OED*) offers the following synonyms for the verb *to sell*: *promote, persuade someone to accept, talk someone into, bring someone around to, win someone over to, win approval for, persuade someone of the merits of.*

Duane Sparks, chairman of the sales training firm The Sales Board, defines *sales* as "the use of one person's communication skills to gain a commitment from another person."

The traditional sales force consists of individuals with the word *sales* in their job titles, but now everyone, at every level, is being encouraged, and in many cases formally trained, to sell every chance they get. One of the major trends in organizations of all kinds is the development of what's known as the "non-traditional sales force." Sparks explains that this concept, which has been talked about for years, is now being taken seriously: "We are amazed at the range of people we are now being asked to train: doctors and nurses, accountants and lawyers, consultants, technicians and engineers, marketers, customer-service reps, product development specialists — you name it!"

In the past, aggressive sales forces were often motivated by many organizations to "sell, sell, sell," without necessarily having to coordinate with those responsible for delivering the product or service being sold. The integration of selling and doing is a healthy development on many levels. For example, at Hillmann Consulting, a national firm engaged in environmental and construction risk management, the staff of environmental scientists and construction engineers are all learning to sell their own services, thereby aligning the accuracy of what they promise with what they can deliver. Founder Chris Hillmann comments on this "seller-doer" model:

For years, our most successful partners became doer-sellers naturally. They manage client relationships, source new contacts, and encourage new business. Of course, "doing" is the first priority of technical staff. We are not trying to make every operations team member into a salesperson. Our focus is on being a true partner to the clients we serve by encouraging our technical professionals to develop relationships and use their expertise to identify opportunities to add value to clients' operations.

We've discovered that the ideal model is a collaboration between our operations team and our business development (BD) teams. If one of our technicians identifies opportunities but is too busy doing the work to effectively follow up, we encourage them to team with local BD personnel. Both groups are essential in providing a superior customer experience and expanding our business. Ultimately, at Hillmann selling is about taking a team approach to anticipating our clients' needs and meeting them in a way that benefits the client!

Effective Selling: Skills Everyone Can Learn

Is the ability to gain commitments from others using communication skills something that everyone can develop?

Yes!

One of the myths about selling effectively is that you must be a particular personality type to excel. The notion, for example, that extroverts are best at sales is a common misconception.

Duane Sparks explains, "Most people, even many within the world of formal sales, believe that a 'natural salesperson' is an extrovert who has a natural gift of gab and can talk endlessly to anyone about any topic. So if you want to 'train' them, all you need is to pump them full of hot air from a motivational speaker."

Sparks, whose company has trained almost half a million salespeople, emphasizes that the skills of effective selling can be developed by people, whatever their social style or Myers-Briggs profile.

What are the most important skills to develop? According to The Sales Board, "On an individual basis, *presentation skills appears to offer the greatest potential for improvement* [my emphasis]."

Whether you are an extrovert, introvert, analytical type, driver, reformer, or peacemaker, presenting is a skill you can learn. And great presentations are a result of making a connection with the audience. When an audience likes you, they are open to being influenced by you. It turns out that the old saying "People buy on emotion and justify with facts" is validated by contemporary research into the principles of influence.

Professional presenters are students of the principles of influence. And even if you think you're not "in sales" or a professional presenter, it's critically important to know the ways in which others are attempting to influence you to buy whatever they're selling. *Influence* is defined by the *OED* as "the capacity or power of persons...to be a compelling force on or produce effects on the actions, behavior, opinions, etc., of others." Or as "the action or process of producing effects on the actions, behavior, opinions, etc., of another or others."

Presentations are exercises in influence. And influence is what powers your ability to sell anything, from automobiles to zucchini. Robert Cialdini, renowned as the "godfather of influence," and the author of the classic work *Influence: The Psychology of Persuasion*, has brought together more than sixty years of research into the science of persuasion and made it accessible and practical. He's discovered that although most people believe they make decisions based on rational analysis, it is actually unconscious, instinctive reactions that determine how we are influenced. Cialdini has identified six universal principles that compel people to say yes to requests. As you learn these principles, you become more aware of your biases, allowing you to make better, wiser decisions. You also become much more effective in your attempts to influence others, bearing in mind the commitment to use all this powerful information for ethical, noble purposes only.

I've aimed to make these six principles more memorable for you by expressing them in the acronym RESALE: reciprocity, engagement, scarcity, authority, liking, and everyone.

Reciprocity

Over the years I've been a guest on many online learning courses and summits, and I recently began my own online endeavor. I confess that at first I was kind of annoyed that we were always asked to offer a "free gift" as part of the effort to motivate people to sign up for these programs. But then I realized that this was one of the essential methods for connecting with people and inspiring them to participate. In the wildly crowded and highly competitive online learning space, if you'd like people to click on your link and sign up for your newsletter, then your free offering invites their nervous system to connect with yours via electronic means. The internet has made the principle of reciprocity clearer than ever — if you want to be successful in this realm, be prepared to give away lots of good stuff. It's just the way the human brain works. Our brains are wired to drive us to return favors, and civilization is largely organized around the principle of reciprocity. After you watch a certain number of helpful free videos on the internet, you'll eventually feel (unless you're a psychopath) compelled to hit the Like button and then the Subscribe button, and then you're on your way to becoming a customer (more on this below when we discuss engagement).

Hare Krishnas have understood this for many years. Once they place a "free" flower in your hand, the chances of your placing some change or bills in their donation box goes up significantly. When you receive a fortune cookie or a mint with your check at a restaurant, you are much more likely to leave a generous tip. The free samples of cheeses or cookies at the grocery store aren't just there to see if you like them; those who enjoy free samples usually buy more groceries. In wine stores, sales go way up when there's a free tasting. In Japan this principle is one of the most salient aspects of the culture. Rituals of reciprocal gift giving and the exchange of favors, known as *giri*, are strong drivers of everyday behavior and serve as the theme for many works of literature, art, and drama.

Cultural anthropologists posit that human societies have been able to survive and thrive by creating "webs of indebtedness" that bind people in cooperative networks, promoting adaptation through interdependent labor, trade, and mutual consideration and support. Giving offers an intrinsic pleasure to healthy humans and inspires the recipient to want to give in return. As Lao Tzu advised, "If you would take, you must first give, this is the beginning of intelligence."

Nicholas A. Christakis, physician and author of *Blueprint: The Evolutionary Origins of a Good Society*, explains, "It is the spread of the good things that vindicates the whole reason we live our lives in networks. If I was always violent to you or gave you germs, you would cut the ties to me and the network would disintegrate. In a deep and fundamental way, networks are connected to goodness, and goodness is required for networks to emerge and spread."

Many professional presenters use the principle of reciprocity effectively to promote their enterprises. Victoria Labalme, a successful keynote speaker, delights her audience members and prospective clients with the clever gift of branded lip balm, which she gives out liberally. Research suggests that the most effective gifts are those that are unexpected, memorable, and personalized. It's one thing if the conference you attend gives everyone a pen, for example, with the conference name and theme on it, but that same gift has much more effect if it has the recipient's name on it as well.

Although there's a strategic and tactical element to reciprocity, the most successful practitioners are those who genuinely focus on the welfare of others but are creative and efficient in the way they provide help and support.

Engagement

Another consistent element of human behavior is that once we engage with a proposition through some form of spoken or written commitment, we are much more likely to follow through with it. In other words, most people's sense of self-worth and identity is tied to the notion that they will be consistent with what they've said or done in the past, especially if they've said or done it in public. Small actions or a few words of affirmation for a proposition organize the nervous system toward future actions and affirmations of a given behavior.

For example, if someone representing a campaign for safe driving knocked on your door and asked you to allow them to erect a large wooden billboard on your front lawn, you, like most of the folks in the study Cialdini cites, would probably decline. But what if ten days earlier someone had stopped by and asked you to place a small postcard for the same campaign in one of the front windows of your home? The people who were engaged in this way first were much more likely to agree to have the billboard erected. By agreeing to place the small card in their window first, the homeowners became engaged with the campaign and were four times more likely to say yes to the signage than those who were asked cold.

The most influential public speakers make consistent use of this principle. One of the simplest ways of doing this is to poll your audience by asking for a show of hands, inviting your audience to engage with a proposition you would like them to affirm. When conducting training sessions, finish by asking people to write down the most important things they've learned and how they intend to apply them; then get them to share what they've learned and their plans for application in small groups; then ask each person to stand up and express their learning and commitment to application. This deepens their engagement with what they've learned, and the public commitment makes it much more likely that they will follow through with it.

Scarcity

It's 2:30 AM and you can't sleep, so you turn on the television and find yourself contemplating purchasing a blanket with sleeves; a can't-miss, get-rich-quick house-flipping or real-estate scheme; a proactive approach to eliminating acne, shredding your abs, or empowering your whole life to fulfill all your dreams and goals; or maybe just a superefficient frying pan grill, slicer-dicer, or Bass-o-Matic. Almost everyone has experienced the hypnotic effect of the infomercial. One aspect of that hypnosis is always an appeal to "act now!" Why? Because "supplies are limited." And, if you place your order in the next fifteen minutes, you'll get "free overnight shipping." Then the ticking clock appears on your screen. Of course, these infomercials run many times a day, for many days, but whatever the product, we always must "act now" so we don't miss out and call within the next fifteen minutes so we don't have to pay for shipping. But wait, there's more! "For a limited time only," we can get two of whatever they are pushing for the price of one, if we "hurry."

It's fun to laugh about this, and *Saturday Night Live* and other shows have had lots of material for satire over the years, but despite the seemingly obvious manipulation, this strategy, appealing to our sense of scarcity, actually works. If it's hard to get, we want it. If there's less of it, we want more of it.

The regions of our brain concerned with survival make us more susceptible to any sales pitch suggesting that supplies are "limited" or "available for a limited time only." The scarcity principle is also commonly known as FOMO: the fear of missing out.

When I began my career as a speaker, and a prospective client would call me to inquire about engaging me, somehow I knew instinctively — an ability most likely inherited from Grandpa Jack — that I needed to act as though I was busy and had to "check my calendar." Of course, this principle has to be applied judiciously and requires good timing and finesse, especially in the realm of dating. Social psychologist Jeremy Nicholson, known as the Attraction Doctor, emphasizes that in relationships, and in business, playing hard to get requires a balancing act: "On the one hand, seeming too eager might be taken as desperate, possibly lowering the perception of your value to a romantic partner. On the other, appearing too aloof could result in that prospect giving up. The key is demonstrating that you are selective — showing a potential partner that they have a unique and special opportunity to be with you, while also providing enough encouragement so they continue their efforts."

Nicholson explains how that same principle is at work in business: "If you communicate to your boss or to a potential employer that you are desperate for an opportunity, they might try to take advantage of you. Acting disinterested, however, may lead them to pass you up for someone who seems more engaged and motivated. Just as in dating, the key is communicating your selectivity but also letting them know you are seriously considering their proposal."

Authority

Whenever you enter a room with other people in it, whether it's a restaurant, an auditorium, or a conference room, part of your brain, the limbic system, is monitoring your status, your place in the social hierarchy. We unconsciously respond to many different signals of status, from a person's height and how symmetrical her face is and how stylish her clothing, to subtler cues like body language and accent. Moreover, the same part of the brain that automatically assesses our status relative to others also compels us to comply with the directions or suggestions of those we perceive to be higher in the hierarchy.

In a wine store, for example, people are much more likely to buy a wine with a "shelf talker" touting a high rating from a recognized critic. Unethical purveyors sometimes use ratings from bogus sources or post a shelf talker praising another vintage besides the one for sale and count on the potential customer's lack of diligence in catching the discrepancy. People tend to follow the lead of those whom other people have deemed expert. This influences behavior in everything from selling fine wine to getting people to commit crimes.

As we discussed in chapter 5, when giving a formal public presentation it's a good idea to have a well-respected, authoritative person introduce you. Authority is also conveyed by the way you dress, stand, and move, your voice tone and choice of words, and most important, by your clarity and presence.

Liking

Many years ago I was swimming in a beautiful pond in southern Virginia on the campus of Sweet Briar College. I thought I was alone until, a few feet away from where I was floating, a woman popped up from below the water and looked around. I guess she thought she had the pond to herself as well, and we both looked surprised. She then looked right at me and inquired, "Friend or foe?" We both laughed and continued to swim.

Just as we assess our status relative to others, we also determine quickly whether they are threats or allies, friends or foes. And when we perceive someone as a friend or potential friend, when we like them, we are much more susceptible to their influence. How do we determine whether someone is likable? Research suggests that this depends on a few key elements, including a sense of commonality. In other words, we tend to like people who are like us and are often suspicious of those who seem different. We also tend to like those who seem to share our goals and values and who demonstrate cooperative behavior, and we are also influenced by positive things that people say about us. Compliments and even obvious flattery often make others more amenable to whatever it is you'd like them to do.

In public speaking the audience determines your likability through a number of different cues, beginning with your body language and voice tonality. If you walk onto the stage or to the front of the room in a relaxed, upright, and confident manner, if you smile and greet the audience in a genuine way, you create the conditions for effective influence.

Psychologist Nalini Ambady showed subjects thirty-second-long videotapes of professors presenting to their classes. The subjects were asked to rate the effectiveness of each teacher after the brief viewing. The results were astonishing — the subjects' ratings, based on what the researchers called *thin-slice judgments*, correlated almost exactly with the ratings obtained from students after a full term of lectures. Further research demonstrated that subjects offered accurate evaluations after viewing video segments less than ten seconds in length. Ambady attributes this remarkable ability to read and instantly interpret body language to "evolutionary adaptation, the need to figure out who friends and foes were."

In addition to walking onstage with a poised, upright posture and a smile, it's a good idea to greet your audience at the beginning of your talk in a sincere and friendly manner. If, for example, you say "good morning" like you mean it, instead of in the formal and dull way that people often do this, and you pause for a moment, people in even the largest audiences will usually respond with a welcoming greeting in return. Then, whenever appropriate, connect with the audience by sharing an observation about something you have in common with them and by complimenting them in a genuine and playful way. (Remember the example from Ankara, Turkey, cited in chapter 4.)

Everyone

If everyone else is doing it, talking about it, or buying it, then our brains make us want to do it, talk about it, or buy it, too. The limbic system drives pack behavior. I call it the principle of "everyone," which is really a variation of the principle of authority. As Cialdini notes, people are more likely to follow through and do the exercises prescribed by a physical therapist who displays her diploma in her office than they are by one who doesn't. Why are we influenced when we see a diploma from a recognizable institution — evidence that a degree or advanced degree has been conferred by that institution? It is because we are experiencing that institution's authority, which is conferred on it by society so that it can confer its authority onto individuals. And the evidence demonstrates that it affects us more than we may realize. People will tend to look to the actions of others for direction or confirmation, especially when they feel uncertain. In Berlin, Germany, it's exceedingly rare for a pedestrian to cross against the traffic light, but in Manhattan almost everyone does it, even many visitors from Berlin, but only after they look around and notice that everyone else is doing it. This is also why your news feed on the social media sites you follow highlights phenomena that are "trending." If it's popular, if everyone is doing it, or if we can be led to believe that everyone's doing it, then our limbic system leads us to feel more comfortable doing it, too, and vice versa.

Nicholson notes that this principle operates in our intimate relationships as well:

> Individuals tend to look at what other people are doing to help provide information about a particular decision, especially when that decision is complex and hard to evaluate, and the choices are unclear. Picking the right romantic partner is one of those complex and confusing decisions. Given that, rather than evaluating all the romantic options available, some daters decide to focus on popular partners as more desirable to them as well (known as Mate Choice Copying). Fortunately you don't need to be a celebrity to have this dynamic work in your favor. For example, just being seen out with an attractive friend (who could possibly be construed as a potential romantic partner), or posting a picture with them on your dating profile, can give your own desirability a boost in the eyes of others, too.

For public speakers this principle means that you will be more effective in generating support for your message, idea,

proposition, or proposal if you can demonstrate that it is popular. In business presentations this principle comes to life in what
companies call "benchmarking" or "best practices." If you can
present data proving that your counterparts in other organizations are doing something that you want your audience to do,
then they are much more likely to do it.

Combining RESALE with PROPAR

If you supercharge RESALE with PROPAR you'll make your
message unforgettably influential. Think of others' needs and
offer something positive and unexpected to inspire reciprocity.
Get them engaged with your proposition. Let them know that it
is special and scarce. Cite research or endorsements from trusted
sources to appeal to the sense of authority. Generate liking by
being friendly, expressing commonalities, and giving compliments. And remember that if you don't know what to order in
a restaurant, your server is trained to respond to your question
about what she recommends by saying: "Well, the *everyone* burger
is our most popular item."

Then, organize your presentation so that you emphasize what
you want the audience to remember at the beginning (primacy),
repeat your key points (repetition), tell a story or do a demonstration (outstanding), and get your audience engaged with questions
real and rhetorical and with examples that are evocative for them
(personal association), and then emphasize your key points with
a call to action at the end (recency).

If the Buddha gave sales presentations, he would be aware of
the ways in which the human mind is conditioned to remember
and be influenced and would always use this understanding with
compassion and a commitment to benefit others.

There's one last secret of mastering the art of public speaking that, more than any other, can help you overcome fear: free yourself from egotism as you prepare to speak. How? There are many different paths and methods, but the simplest is to form an intention and express it. This is sometimes called prayer, but it doesn't have to be religious. Find an invocation that works best for you to facilitate a sense of surrendering the ego and aligning with a higher purpose.

My favorite pre-presentation invocation comes from *A Course in Miracles*:

> You can do much on behalf of your own healing and that of others if, in a situation calling for help, you think of it this way:
> *I am here only to be truly helpful.*
> *I am here to represent Him Who sent me.*
> *I do not have to worry about what to say or what to do, because He Who sent me will direct me.*
> *I am content to be wherever He wishes, knowing He goes there with me.*
> *I will be healed as I let Him teach me to heal.*

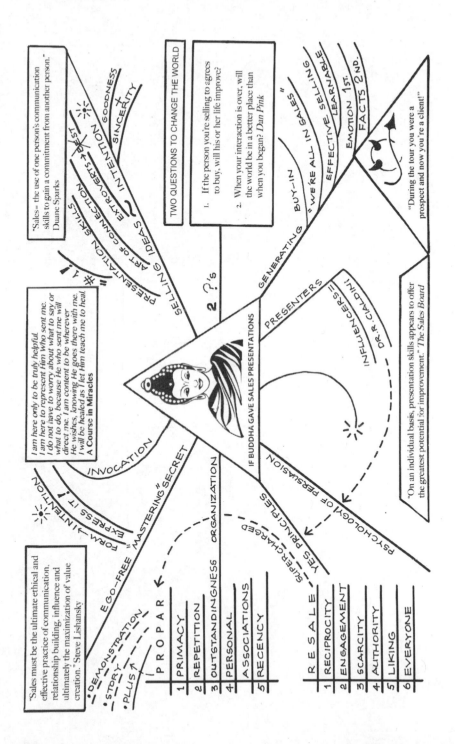

"Sales= the use of one person's communication skills to gain a commitment from another person." Duane Sparks

GOODNESS
SINCERITY
INTENTION
EXTROVERTS BEST
IDEAS
ART OF CONNECTION
PRESENTATION SKILLS
#1!
SELLING

TWO QUESTIONS TO CHANGE THE WORLD

1. If the person you're selling to agrees to buy, will his or her life improve?
2. When your interaction is over, will the world be in a better place than when you began? *Dan Pink*

GENERATING BUY-IN
"WE'RE ALL IN SALES"
EFFECTIVE SELLING
LEARNABLE
EMOTION 1ST.
FACTS 2ND.

"During the tour you were a prospect and now you're a client!"

2 ?'s

I am here only to be truly helpful.
I am here to represent Him Who sent me.
I do not have to worry about what to say or what to do, because He who sent me will direct me. I am content to be wherever He wishes, knowing He goes there with me.
I will be healed as I let Him teach me to heal.
A Course in Miracles

PRESENTERS
INFLUENCERS =
DR. CIALDINI
IF BUDDHA GAVE SALES PRESENTATIONS
PSYCHOLOGY OF PERSUASION

"On an individual basis, presentation skills appears to offer the greatest potential for improvement." *The Sales Board*

INVOCATION
FORM → INTENTION
EXPRESS IT !
EGO-FREE "MASTERING" SECRET
ORGANIZATION
SUPERCHARGED
YES PRINCIPLES

"Sales must be the ultimate ethical and effective practice of communication, relationship building, influence and ultimately the maximization of value creation." Steve Lishansky

• DEMONSTRATION
• STORY
• PLUS ↑

P R O P A R
1 PRIMACY
2 REPETITION
3 OUTSTANDINGNESS
4 PERSONAL
5 ASSOCIATIONS
   RECENCY

R E S A L E
1 RECIPROCITY
2 ENGAGEMENT
3 SCARCITY
4 AUTHORITY
5 LIKING
6 EVERYONE

Conclusion

The Master's Secret Mirror

*In the master's secret mirror, even at the moment of highest re-
nown and accomplishment, there is an image of the newest student in class, eager for knowledge, willing to play the fool.*

— GEORGE LEONARD,
Mastery: The Keys to Success and Long-Term Fulfillment

Just before he died, the great artist Auguste Renoir completed
his final painting. Although he suffered from paralyzing ar-
thritis and had to have the brush taped to his hand in order to
work, he persevered. In his final days he reflected, "I think I'm
beginning to understand something about painting." Renoir pos-
sessed the essential quality characteristic of all true masters — a
lifelong commitment to learning.

The more knowledge and experience you have in a given
area, the easier it becomes to learn more. At the same time, as
your knowledge and experience increase, so does your awareness
of the vast amount that remains to be learned. This is why the
wise are always humble.

Whatever your current level as a public speaker, there is always room to improve. Every presentation you deliver, and each
one that you witness, offers an opportunity for learning. Practice
every chance you get. Tell stories and jokes to friends. Give informal talks to anyone who will listen. Join your local Toastmasters

or other speaker or storytelling club, or take an evening class in public speaking.

Here is an amazing technique for accelerating your progress.

Apply the High-Performance Feedback Protocol

Consider how a baby learns. They absorb all the data they can with enthusiasm and wonder, instantly translating mistakes into learning experiences and thus learning at remarkable speed without losing self-confidence. Cultivate this same high-performance learning attitude while seeking feedback on your presentations.

What kind of impact do you have on an audience? If appropriate, hand out evaluation forms, ask questions of audience members, or invite trusted friends or colleagues to attend your presentations for the purpose of giving you detailed feedback. An accurate critique is the greatest gift you can receive. Ideally, find a trusted friend or colleague who shares your commitment to continual improvement. Arrange to attend each other's presentations, or if that's not possible, watch videos of them. Plan a time to meet and exchange feedback, and use the following procedure.

Ask your partner to begin by focusing only on those aspects of your presentation that, in his opinion, could be improved. The feedback should be specific, actionable, direct, and honest. When receiving your critique, be receptive — take notes and don't explain or defend yourself. Ask questions only to gain further clarity. This form of listening allows you to get unusually pure feedback. Once the focus on your areas for improvement has been completed, your partner will then give you feedback, this time focusing on your strengths. Again, listen without responding so you can gain a full appreciation and understanding of what you did well. After completing the feedback on areas for improvement and areas of strength, enjoy an open, exploratory creative conversation about what you may do differently next time.

This exercise is tremendously powerful, and if you practice it faithfully, with a perceptive and sensitive partner, it will lead you to insights about your presentations that otherwise would be elusive. As you develop skill in critiquing your partner's presentation, you become more discerning and attuned to what works and what doesn't in public speaking.

I was able to elevate my skills dramatically as a result of the feedback I received and gave practicing this protocol with Tony Buzan. We taught together for years and gave each other feedback after every class or keynote speech.

You can also apply this high-performance approach with a team. When I lead presentation skills seminars, each of the participants gets videotaped as they present so they can see the before and after. In a recent class we had twelve people, and we followed a simple but powerful protocol that I invite you to try with your team. We asked each person to set the scene and explain the context in which they would be presenting. We all aimed to watch and then later give feedback from the perspective of the audience that would actually be receiving the talk.

In this most recent class, held for a construction management firm in New York, half the people were practicing sales presentations, and the other half were supervisors and foremen practicing speaking to workers on job sites about the company's new safety initiative. Each person presented in turn, with a time limit of five minutes, and we went through all the presentations. After a break, we watched the videos and shared feedback on each presentation.

First, we asked the person giving the presentation to critique themselves and if necessary, and it often is, we coached them on giving themselves critical but supportive feedback. Although many people were quite harsh in their self-assessments, they were also reasonably accurate in their analysis of what they might improve. After the self-critique, the rest of the class was invited to give feedback to the presenter. Again, they received coaching on how to give the most useful feedback. This usually involves helping people translate from generalities into specifics and from evaluations into observations.

Specifics and observations are usually more constructive than generalities and evaluations. To tell someone, "You sounded indecisive and unsure of yourself" or "You are a slob" is not as useful or constructive as "You said 'like' and 'you know' eleven times" or "Your shirttail was hanging out, and your shoes weren't shined."

The person receiving the feedback just listened and took notes without commentary. After all the feedback on areas of improvement was given, we asked the presenter to analyze the strengths of their presentation. Although most people are able to critique themselves, they're surprisingly inept when it comes to realizing and acknowledging their strengths. So we asked the group to share what they perceived as the strengths of the presenter and to articulate what they appreciated about each person. We encouraged the presenter to be receptive and to take notes on this appreciative feedback and to limit the response to just saying, "Thank you." This exchange is often quite moving since many folks, especially those in field-operations positions, have never received this kind of public appreciation.

It is useful to learn your specific areas for improvement, but if you're like most people, you'll find that the greatest benefit of the feedback process is to *discover your strong points*.

As the class proceeded the participants began to recognize that they were creating an environment, rare in many workplaces, where they can give and receive feedback in a manner designed to bring out their best, in a framework of unconditional support for their self-expression. After each person received feedback, we had a creative dialogue about how they might integrate the feedback and rework the presentation, and then after some time for Mind Mapping and rehearsal, each person was videotaped for the second time. The transformation based on this process is often remarkable.

A construction site supervisor named Vinnie offers a powerful example. In Vinnie's first presentation on safety he tried his best to explain the benefits of the program based on the talking points provided by the external firm that did the company's safety training. He said "um" and "ah" between almost every phrase, and despite being an imposing figure at six foot two and 290 pounds, his rocking movements and fidgeting compromised his stature and his presence. Yet, despite all that, the group could feel that Vinnie actually cared about safety and the well-being of his workers. The feedback he received was essentially, "Please don't try so hard to give a presentation and instead just tell your story."

In his second attempt, Vinnie began by pausing and making deep eye contact with everyone in the room before beginning his story. The group was immediately engaged by his presence. Vinnie went on to tell us about his father, who was his hero. Vinnie's dad was a site supervisor, and as a result of someone's carelessness on the job, he was hit with a wrecking ball and suffered devastating injuries that forced him to go on disability for years. Holding back tears, Vinnie shared the impact this had on his family and how it shaped his own passion for safety. Everyone in the room was completely transfixed, and Vinnie's story went straight to the gut in a way that generated passion, rather than just compliance, for the new safety initiative.

My wish for you is that this book will fire your passion for public speaking while giving you the practical knowledge and methods you need to translate that passion into mastery. Before I began my career as a public speaker, while still training as a teacher of the Alexander Technique, I read a book entitled *Zen in the Art of Archery*, written by a German philosophy professor who studied the Japanese discipline of Kyudo, "The Way of the Bow." It captured my imagination with notions of perfecting the "artless art" and the suggestion that the marksman "aim at himself." That sounded so cool, but what does it mean? I wasn't really interested in Japanese archery beyond its value as a metaphor, so how to transfer the meaning into life? Another passage from the book has stayed with me for all these years. "You can learn from an ordinary bamboo leaf what ought to happen. It bends lower and lower under the weight of snow. Suddenly the snow slips to the ground without the leaf having stirred."

The author is describing what Csíkszentmihályi calls *flow*. The arrow "must fall from the archer like snow from a bamboo leaf, before he even thinks it." That's what it feels like in the Flow State when you are presenting to a group. The "weight of snow" is the pressure of the moment, and your words will fall effortlessly into the hearts and minds of your audience if you prepare properly.

"The best moments in our lives are not the passive, receptive, relaxing times," Csíkszentmihályi explains. "The best moments usually occur when a person's body or mind is stretched to its limits in a voluntary effort to accomplish something difficult and worthwhile." If you apply the eight secrets we've explored, you'll discover that some of the best moments of your life will be in front of a meeting room or up on the stage.

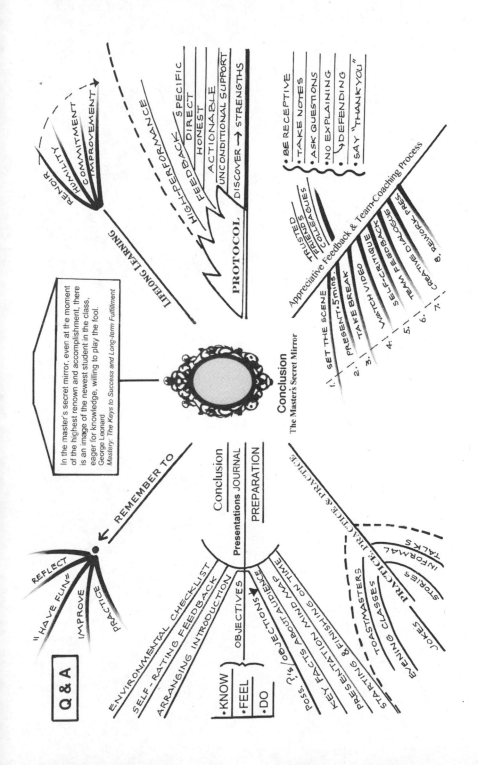

Conclusion
The Master's Secret Mirror

In the master's secret mirror, even at the moment of the highest renown and accomplishment, there is an image of the newest student in the class, eager for knowledge, willing to play the fool.
George Leonard
Mastery: The Keys to Success and Long-term Fulfillment

LIFELONG LEARNING

RENOWN
HUMILITY
COMMITMENT
IMPROVEMENT

HIGH-PERFORMANCE FEEDBACK
SPECIFIC
DIRECT
HONEST
ACTIONABLE
UNCONDITIONAL SUPPORT
DISCOVER → STRENGTHS

PROTOCOL

BE RECEPTIVE
TAKE NOTES
ASK QUESTIONS
NO EXPLAINING
DEFENDING
SAY "THANK YOU"

Appreciative Feedback & Team-Coaching Process

1. SET THE SCENE
2. PRESENT. 5 mins.
3. TAKE BREAK
4. WATCH VIDEO
5. SELF-CRITIQUE
6. TEAM DIALOGUES
7. CREATIVE PRESS
8. RE-WORK

TRUSTED
FRIENDS
COLLEAGUES

REMEMBER TO

REFLECT
"HAVE FUN"
IMPROVE
PRACTICE

Q & A

ENVIRONMENTAL CHECKLIST
SELF-RATING & FEEDBACK
ARRANGING INTRODUCTION

Conclusion

Presentations JOURNAL

PREPARATION

OBJECTIVES

• KNOW
• FEEL
• DO

Q's/OBJECTIONS
POSS. FACTS about AUDIENCE
FINISHING ON MIND ON TIME
KEY FACTS
PRESENTATION & FIELD
STARTING TOASTMASTERS
EVENING CLASSES
JOKES
STORIES
INFORMAL TALKS

PRACTICE, PRACTICE & PRACTICE

Questions and Answers

What should I do if I draw a blank in the middle of my presentation?

If you have prepared thoroughly for your presentation, you won't experience this very often. However, even the best-prepared presenters occasionally experience a sudden loss of place or a mental block. Your strength will lie in how you handle the situation. When you recognize that you have lost your place, pause for a moment, exhale, and collect yourself. If your train of thought does not return, you can simply ask your audience, "Where was I?" — at which point someone in the group will undoubtedly respond. This kind of honesty and directness will enhance your rapport with the audience.

How much time should I devote to rehearsing a presentation?

There is no set minimum or maximum amount of time — rehearse until you feel confident. Set your objectives, then generate, organize, and become comfortable with your material, as soon as you can. This will give you more time to experiment with creative ways to deliver your message. The key to effective rehearsal is to begin informally as soon as you know that you are giving a presentation. For example, as I'm writing this, I know that I will be giving a new presentation to an important client about two months from now. We are still not sure if it will be delivered in person or live online, and I'm preparing for both possibilities. I'm still working on my Mind Map for the presentation and I'm playing with some images for my PowerPoint, but I'm envisioning connecting with the audience and playing with ways of getting my message through to them. The details of the presentation will come together effortlessly as I play with the ideas I have each day and share what I'm thinking with my wife.

What if I have to give a presentation on very short notice?

Use Mind Mapping to generate ideas and organize your content after you set your objectives, then practice the Mind Map memory method. Get out of the CAN and give yourself a DOSE in the ways we covered in chapter 7.

What should I remember when making presentations to people more senior than I?

Remember that you have been invited to address them for a reason. Generally, the more senior people are, the better they respond to those who conduct themselves in a respectful but authoritative manner. Never apologize for being there. Make sure that you dress immaculately and, if necessary, visualize how everyone in your audience looked in their first-grade class photos.

If for some reason beyond my control I am confronted with an unfavorable environment (too hot, stuffy, poor lighting,

etc.) for my presentation, what can I do to make the best of the situation?

If the environment is unfavorable, and there is nothing you can do to change it, acknowledge this in a lighthearted way, and give your group more frequent breaks.

What are the most common mistakes presenters make?

Not preparing. Molecule fondling. Apologizing. Speaking in a monotone. Going on too long. Overselling (being insensitive to the moment when your audience is sold and going on beyond that point instead of asking for the sale).

How can I handle difficult people?

Most difficult people are difficult because they have a problem. Often it has nothing to do with you and your presentation. Some people are insecure and like to show off their knowledge, others may have been stuck in traffic that morning or are dealing with digestive difficulties. A few may actually be reacting to some aspect of your presentation. These problems can manifest themselves in anything from noisy paper shuffling to unnecessary or hostile questions. The best way to address such situations is, first of all, not to take them personally.

When handling aggressive questions, listen carefully and find something in what the questioner is saying that you can agree with; avoid getting defensive. The better you are at empathizing, the easier it will be to defuse the situation. Don't let yourself get caught in a battle, even if you are sure you can overwhelm your "opponent" with superior knowledge. You may win the battle but lose your audience. If you maintain your rapport with the audience, you will find that they will be effectively self-policing and not tolerating significant disruption by a disgruntled member.

Jerry Seinfeld offers sage advice on dealing with awkward audience members:

> Very early on in my career, I hit upon this idea of being the Heckle Therapist. So that when people would say something nasty, I would immediately become very sympathetic to them and try to help them with their problem and try to work out what was upsetting them, and try to be very understanding with their anger. It opened up this whole fun avenue for me as a comedian, and no one had ever seen that before....Instead of fighting them, I would say "You seem so upset, and I know that's not what you wanted to have happen tonight. Let's talk about your problem" and the audience would find it funny and it would really discombobulate the heckler too, because I wouldn't go against them, I would take their side.

Finally, bear in mind that if you are well prepared and present yourself with confidence and authority, these kinds of problems will rarely arise.

Can you give me some guidance on answering questions?

Always listen carefully for the essence of what is being asked, and treat every questioner with respect. Make sure that the question is heard by everyone, and repeat it if necessary. Pause and think before answering. Answer concisely. If you do not know the answer, you can refer the question to the group. This is often a good idea even when you do know the answer, since it encourages group involvement. Otherwise say, "I don't know," with authority, and offer to seek the answer and provide it at some future time.

How should I use humor?

Never use humor. *Just kidding!* Laughter generates endorphins and defuses stress, helping you and your audience to relax. Cultivate appropriate lightheartedness, and avoid taking yourself too seriously. If you want to tell a joke, practice it and work on the timing, and be sure that it relates to what you want people to remember.

How will improving my presentation skills affect other aspects of my life?

Mastering the art of public speaking will help you grow as a human being. You learn to place your ego on the shelf as you actively seek feedback on your performance and as you transform your fears, insecurities, and limiting habits.

You will gain valuable insights into your own nature and into that of others. These insights will help you develop your skills in leadership and personal relationships and will enhance your self-confidence, poise, and sense of personal power.

How can I learn the Alexander Technique?

The Alexander Technique is best learned through individual lessons with a qualified teacher. Lessons usually last from thirty to forty-five minutes. Most teachers recommend a basic course of at least thirty lessons. Alexander work is the single most powerful method for transforming your fear and supercharging your career as a public speaker.

What about presenting as part of a group?

When I was a professional juggler our code was "Always make your partners look good." In the theater, you'll notice that in a well-directed and well-performed production the ensemble is always positioned and focused to direct attention to the featured performer at any given moment. This applies to group presentations and is especially important in business settings.

If you're aiming to be hired as a team, clients will assess how you interact with one another. It makes a much more positive impression on the audience when those onstage, or in front of the room, demonstrate that they are actively listening to colleagues who are presenting together. When the audience observes co-presenter body language that expresses interest — upright posture, affirmative head nodding, and so on — their mirror neurons compel them to do the same. But if your CEO is checking her email or slouching and looking out the window while the CMO is speaking, the effect can be disastrous. Also, observe as co-presenters change over from one speaker to another. Is there an awkward moment when they almost collide on the way off or on the stage, or is the transition accomplished gracefully? A simple rule is that the person finishing yields to the person who has just been introduced. All business presentations are theater, so always make your partners look good, and rehearse your exits and entrances — and everything in between.

And if you speak at conferences, apply this idea to the whole event. If you come after someone else on the schedule, do your homework and discover something about them or their message that you can highlight and link to your presentation. If someone is speaking after you, you'll make friends and be beloved by the conference sponsors if you say something that raises interest in and anticipation for the next speaker.

What has changed in the world of public speaking since you began your career?

Attention spans are shorter, dress codes are more casual, audiences are more global and diverse, and overhead projectors are obsolete. And we are at the dawn of the age of virtual presentation. In a 2010 episode of the television show *The Big Bang Theory*, Sheldon Cooper appears via a Mobile Virtual Presence Device (MVPD), a robot he invented to protect him from life's dangers. Decorated with one of his shirts, the MVPD, a.k.a. the Shelbot, uses a webcam, loudspeakers, a flat-panel display, and a movable platform to allow the germophobic Sheldon to interact with his friends at a sterile distance. I remember thinking when I saw that episode that it wouldn't be too long before a similar phenomenon might arise at conferences. In 2018 I gave a keynote at the Exponential Medicine conference sponsored by Singularity University, and one of the other speakers onstage in front of an audience of eight hundred was the virtual presence of futurist and author of *The Age of Spiritual Machines*, Ray Kurzweil.

What are some of the specific challenges of speaking via a virtual modality?

In recent years, I've led many seminars via virtual, online platforms and have given more keynotes this way as well. The biggest challenge is that it is harder to read the audience since, in larger events, most of them aren't visible on the screen and most are muted so it's not always easy to know if everyone is laughing at the jokes, nodding in agreement, dozing off, or checking their email. The other challenges are technical. It takes some practice to develop skill in using visuals appropriately and to move people in and out of breakout sessions. I can say, with full confidence, that everything we have covered in this book becomes even more important when you are presenting virtually.

What are the biggest mistakes you have made in your career as a speaker?

My biggest mistake was in my very first paid presentation, for a group of bankers in England in 1978. I took the presentation too lightly and wasn't properly prepared. I vowed that would never happen again. It hasn't. Fortunately, most of my presentations since then have been well received because I've sincerely applied everything I've written about. And in reviewing the feedback I've received over the years, it's become clear that the cause of my least successful presentations is indulgence in molecule fondling, getting so caught up in my passion for a subject that it overshadows my empathy for the audience. *Hoisted*, as Shakespeare notes, *on my own petard.*

Keeping a Presentation Journal

After experiencing the high-performance presentation feedback protocol a few times, most groups can internalize it and can begin using it on their own. It becomes part of the culture, with the added benefit that people learn how to give and receive feedback in realms beyond just presentation skills.

As part of the protocol we also invite everyone to keep a presentation journal to help plan and evaluate presentations. If you and other members of your group keep a presentation journal, you can supercharge the feedback process. Here's how.

Use your journal to record information about the audience, your objectives, the environment, and your content before you give your talk. After each presentation, objectively evaluate your strengths and areas for improvement, and record them.

You can use the following as a guide for building your owncomprehensive high-performance presentation journal. Reviewing your journal regularly will help you to hone your high-performance attitude and speed your progress.

Preparation

Use this section for preparing for your presentation, then afterward review it and add your comments. You may include:

A Mind Map of your presentation

Key facts about the audience (number of people, expectations, gender, etc.)

Objectives for this presentation (know, feel, do)

Possible questions or objections from the audience

Starting and finishing time

Logistics for arranging the introduction

Other logistics

A complete environmental checklist, as shown on the next page

ELEMENT	COMMENTS
Lighting	
Air quality/temperature	
Furniture	
Microphone	
AV equipment	
Music	
Plants	
Flowers	
Acoustics	
Warming up exercises (space/time arranged?)	
Miscellaneous	

Feedback

Record your comments and, where appropriate, rate yourself in each area on a scale from 1 to 10.

Objectives accomplished   1 2 3 4 5 6 7 8 9 10
Comments:

Use of audiovisuals   1 2 3 4 5 6 7 8 9 10
Comments:

Posture   1 2 3 4 5 6 7 8 9 10
Comments:

Gestures   1 2 3 4 5 6 7 8 9 10
Comments:

Movement   1 2 3 4 5 6 7 8 9 10
Comments:

Voice   1 2 3 4 5 6 7 8 9 10
Comments:

Overall body language   1 2 3 4 5 6 7 8 9 10
Comments:

Major areas for improvement of my presentation:

_____

Major strengths:

_____

What would I do differently next time?

_____

My own comfort and enjoyment level:

_____

General comments:

_____

Keep your journal in a special file, along with your Mind Maps and any evaluation forms you receive. Even if you don't record this information, you can still benefit by asking yourself the journal questions after each presentation. Practice, reflect, improve, enjoy, and have fun.

If you want more support, consider joining your local Toastmasters club or the National Speakers Association. And here's one last practice that will help you master the art of public speaking: Prepare and deliver a presentation on this book, or, if that feels too daunting, begin with a talk on your favorite chapter. Start by making your own Mind Maps — you can, of course, use the maps in the book for inspiration — and then find an audience to inspire. If you're really inspired, make a video of your talk, and post it on the link you will find at michaelgelb.com/resources. I will curate community reviews so you can get feedback.

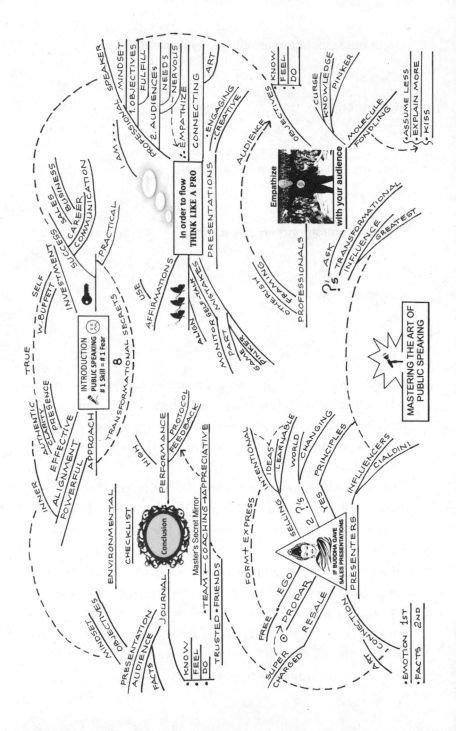

MASTERING THE ART OF PUBLIC SPEAKING

In order to flow THINK LIKE A PRO

PROFESSIONAL MINDSET
1. OBJECTIVES — FULFILL
2. AUDIENCES — NEEDS
I AM — NERVOUS
Empathize
Connecting — ART
Creative — Engaging
Presentations
Audience
Framing — OTHERISH
PINKER — GAME
PART
6 PINKER
MONITOR SELF-TALK
ALIGN SELF-TALK
USE
AFFIRMATIONS

Empathize **with your audience**
OBJECTIVES • KNOW • FEEL • DO
CURSE KNOWLEDGE
PINKER
MOLECULE FONDLING
→ ASSUME LESS
• EXPLAIN MORE
• KISS
Ask Q's
TRANSFORMATIONAL
INFLUENCE
GREATEST
PROFESSIONALS

INTRODUCTION
PUBLIC SPEAKING
1 Skill = # 1 Fear
8 TRANSFORMATIONAL SECRETS

PRACTICAL
COMMUNICATION
CAREER
SALES
BUSINESS
SUCCESS
INVESTMENT
W. BUFFETT
SELF
TRUE
AUTHENTIC
INNER
CLARITY
EFFECTIVE
PRESENCE
ALIGNMENT
POWERFUL
APPROACH

SPEAKER

CONCLUSION
ENVIRONMENTAL CHECKLIST
PERFORMANCE
HIGH
PROTOCOL
FEEDBACK
Master's Secret Mirror
COACHING → APPRECIATIVE
TEAM
TRUSTED • FRIENDS
JOURNAL
MINDSET
OBJECTIVES
PRESENTATION
AUDIENCE
FACTS
KNOW
FEEL
DO

FORM + EXPRESS
INTENTIONAL
IDEAS
LEARNABLE
SELLING
WORLD
CHANGING
Q's
YES
PRINCIPLES
INFLUENCERS
CIALDINI
PRESENTERS
FREE EGO
→ PRO PAR
SUPER CHARGED
RESALE
CONNECTION
ART
• EMOTION 1ST
• FACTS 2ND

IF BUDDHA GAVE SALES PRESENTATIONS

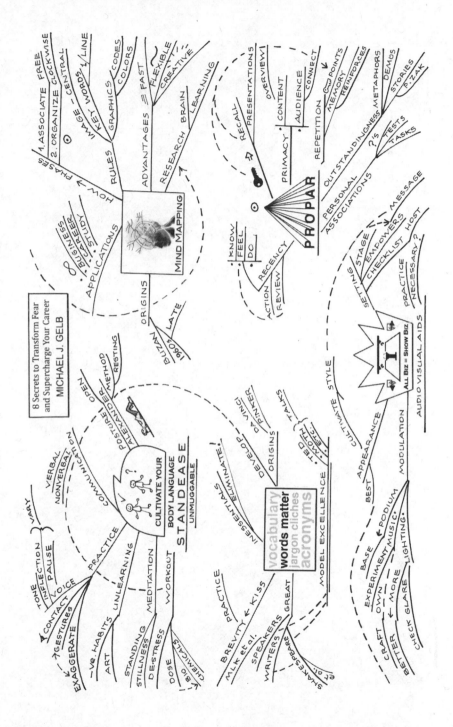

8 Secrets to Transform Fear and Supercharge Your Career
MICHAEL J. GELB

MIND MAPPING

- Advantages = FAST
  - Flexible
  - Creative
- Research Brain
- Learning
- Rules
  - 1. Associate Free
  - 2. Organize Clockwise ☉
  - Image - Central
  - Key Words 1/Line
  - Graphics
  - Colors
  - Codes
- How ∞ Phases
- Applications
  - Study
  - Career
  - Business
- Origins
  - Buzan 1960's
  - Late

PROPAR

- Recall
  - Presentations
    - Overview
    - Primacy • Content
    - Audience • Connect
- Repetition
  - Memory Points
  - Reinforces
  - Metaphors
  - Stories
  - P-Zak
  - Demos
- Outstandingness
  - ?'s
  - Tests
  - Tasks
- Personal Associations
- Know Feel Do
- Recency
  - Action / Review
- Setting Stage
  - Empowers
  - Checklist
  - Message
  - Host
  - Practice
  - Necessary ?
- All Biz = Show Biz
  - Audio Visual Aids
  - Appearance
    - Best
    - Experiment
    - Base
    - Own
    - Podium
    - Music
    - Craft
    - Better
    - More Lighting
    - Check Glare
  - Cultivate Style
  - Modulation

CULTIVATE YOUR BODY LANGUAGE

STANDEASE
UNMUGGABLE

- Communication
  - Open
  - Posture
  - Alexander Method
  - Resting
  - Verbal
  - Nonverbal
    - Tone
    - Inflection Vary
    - Pause
    - Voice
  - Practice
    - Contact
    - Gestures
    - Exaggerate
    - Eye
    - Chemicals
      - Bio
      - Dose
      - De-stress
      - Workout
      - Meditation
      - Stillness
      - Standing
      - Art
      - Habits Unlearning
      - Re-

vocabulary words matter
jargon cliches
acronyms

- Model Excellence
  - Shakespeare
  - Writers
  - Great
  - Speakers
  - MLK et al.
  - Brevity → KISS
  - Practice
- Origins
  - Develop Vinci Thinker
  - Talks
  - Truth / Emote
  - Inessentials Eliminate!

Acknowledgments

Tony Buzan, to whom this book is dedicated, convened regular meetings of his think tank, known as the Learning Methods Group, from 1975 to 1980. The meetings usually took place at Tony's home in the London village of Hampstead or at a nearby Chinese restaurant in Golders Green and featured lively discussions and debates about the nature of mind, art, science, philosophy, and how to develop human potential. The group included a number of individuals who went on to become successful authors, artists, thought leaders, business consultants, and public speakers, including Peter Russell, Mark Brown, and Brian Weller.

In January 2020, after enjoying five days at the Alexander Technique retreat in California that I have attended annually since 1979, I went to Tiburon to spend a few days with friends before going on to teach at the Esalen Institute. On the way to Tiburon I received a telephone message, and although the number was unfamiliar, I immediately recognized the sonorous voice on my voice mail from forty years past: it was Brian Weller's. As serendipity arranged, Brian wasn't far from my friend's place, and we enjoyed a reunion that proved to be much more than just a glorious festival of reminiscence; it also led to the renewal of our creative collaboration, manifesting directly in his amazing illustrations for this book. I'm grateful to the Universe for reconnecting us, and to Brian for his masterful contribution to this book.

I'm also grateful to:

My Alexander Technique colleagues, especially Beret Arcaya, Caren Bayer, Michael Frederick, and Stacy Siena.

Thought leaders in the fields of influence, sales, and linguistics, including Robert Cialdini, Tammy Gales, Steve Lishansky, Harvey Mackay, Jeremy Nicholson, Dan Pink, Steven Pinker, and Duane Sparks.

All the wonderful people who contributed to this book, including Ed Bassett, Vanda North, Jim D'Agostino, Joan and Sandy Gelb, Chris Hillmann, Peter Russell, and Eva Selhub.

The marvelous team at New World Library, including Jason Gardner, Kristen Cashman, Tona Pearce Myers, Tanya Fox, Mimi Kusch, and Monique Muhlenkamp.

The amazing, incomparable Deborah Domanski.

Notes

Introduction: The #1 Fear Is the #1 Skill

p. 1   *"Invest in yourself"*: Catherine Clifford, "Billionaire Warren
Buffett: This Is the 'One Easy Way' to Increase Your Worth
by 'At Least' 50 Percent," CNBC.com, December 5, 2018,
https://www.cnbc.com/2018/12/05/warren-buffett-how-to
-increase-your-worth-by-50-percent.html.

p. 3   *"Bureaucracy defends the status quo"*: Laurence J. Peter, *Peter's
Quotations: Ideas for Our Time* (New York: Collins Reference,
1977), 83. See also Rodd Wagner, "New Evidence the Peter
Principle Is Real — And What to Do about It," *Forbes*, April 10,
2018, https://www.forbes.com/sites/roddwagner/2018/04/10
/new-evidence-the-peter-principle-is-real-and-what-to-do
-about-it/#52658d281809.

p. 4   *"My devotion to continuous improvement of my communication"*:
personal communication with the author, circa 1988.

p. 5   *"If you have ever thought that you would rather die"*: Kaya Burgess,
"Speaking in Public Is Worse Than Death for Most," *Times of
London*, science section, October 30, 2013, https://www.thetimes
.co.uk/article/speaking-in-public-is-worse-than-death-for-most
-5l2bvqlmbnt.

p. 5   *Many surveys rank public speaking*: Christopher Ingraham, "America's Top Fears: Public Speaking, Heights, and Bugs," *The Washington Post*, October 30, 2014, https://www.washingtonpost.com/news/wonk/wp/2014/10/30/clowns-are-twice-as-scary-to-democrats-as-they-are-to-republicans. See also Karen Kangas Dwyer and Marlina M. Davidson, "Is Public Speaking Really More Feared Than Death?," *Communication Research Reports* 29, no. 2 (2012): 99–107, https://www.tandfonline.com/doi/full/10.1080/08824096.2012.667772?scroll=top&needAccess=true.

p. 6   *"When faced with standing up in front of a group"*: Glenn Croston, "The Thing We Fear More Than Death," *Psychology Today*, November 29, 2012, https://www.psychologytoday.com/us/blog/the-real-story-risk/201211/the-thing-we-fear-more-death.

p. 7   *Gordon Goodman, a successful actor and singer*: Andrew Salomon, "Study Shows Stage Fright Is Common Among Working Actors," *Backstage*, September 21, 2011, https://www.backstage.com/magazine/article/study-shows-stage-fright-common-among-working-actors-60640.

p. 9   *"What Gandhi thinks, what he feels"*: Desai, quoted in Eknath Easwaran, *Gandhi the Man: How One Man Changed Himself to Change the World*, 4th ed. (Tomales, CA: Nilgiri Press, 2011), 114.

p. 10   *We don't develop or increase our authenticity*: Jennifer Beer, "The Inconvenient Truth about Your 'Authentic' Self," *Scientific American* (blog), March 5, 2020, https://blogs.scientificamerican.com/observations/the-inconvenient-truth-about-your-authentic-self.

p. 10   *"These are my new shoes"*: Charles Barkley, television commercial for Nike, YouTube video, https://www.youtube.com/watch?v=ev2kYHXma5I.

p. 11   *In his classic* On Becoming a Leader: Warren Bennis, *On Becoming a Leader*, 4th ed. (New York: Basic Books, 2009).

Chapter 1: In Order to Flow, Think Like a Pro

p. 13   *what psychologist Mihály Csíkszentmihályi describes as* flow: Mihály Csíkszentmihályi, *Flow: The Psychology of Optimal Experience* (New York: Harper Perennial, 2008).

p. 19   *"The brain doesn't pay attention to boring things"*: John Medina, *Brain Rules: 12 Principles for Surviving and Thriving at Work, Home, and School* (Seattle: Pear Press, 2009), 93.

p. 20   *"learning to write is like negotiating an obstacle course in boot camp"*: Steven Pinker, *The Sense of Style: The Thinking Person's Guide to Writing in the 21st Century* (New York: Penguin, 2015), 12.

Chapter 2: Empathize with Your Audience

p. 26   *for most people that's the limit*: George A. Miller, "The Magical Number Seven, Plus or Minus Two: Some Limits on Our Capacity for Processing Information," *Psychological Review* 101, no. 2 (1956): 343–52.

p. 29   *Shor liked to conduct informal market research by pretending*: Harvey Mackay's webpage, accessed April 23, 2020, https://harvey mackay.com.

p. 30   *"Think like a wise man but communicate in the language of the people"*: W.B. Yeats, quote on the cover of *W.B. Yeats, The Short Stories* (Miniature Masterpieces, 2013).

p. 31   *"the curse of knowledge"*: Steven Pinker, *The Sense of Style: The Thinking Person's Guide to Writing in the 21st Century* (New York: Penguin, 2015), 63.

p. 35   *"It's no secret that the founders of start-ups"*: Keith McFarland, "The Psychology of Success," *Inc.*, November 1, 2005, https://www.inc .com/magazine/20051101/spotlight-psychology.html.

p. 37   *like writing a love letter and addressing it to Occupant*: Based on a witticism widely attributed to AT&T presentation research manager Ken Haemer, who used the punch line "To whom it may concern."

Chapter 3: Use Mind Maps to Generate, Organize, and Remember Your Message

p. 51   *"I was exposed to various alternative note-taking modalities"*: Jim D'Agostino, personal communication with the author, February 14, 2020.

Chapter 4: PROPAR

p. 60   *Psychologists call this the* primacy effect: *APA Dictionary of Psychology*, s.v. "primacy effect," accessed April 23, 2020, https://dictionary.apa.org/primacy-effects.

p. 66   *"I knew the truth — perhaps I alone"*: Neil LaBute, "Rabbit Candle," Significant Objects, December 1, 2009, http://significantobjects .com/2009/12/01/rabbit-candle.

p. 69   *"My experiments show that character-driven stories"*: Paul J. Zak, "Why Your Brain Loves Good Storytelling," *Harvard Business Review*, October 28, 2014, https://hbr.org/2014/10/why-your -brain-loves-good-storytelling.

p. 71   *The Recency Effect: APA Dictionary of Psychology*, s.v. "recency effect," accessed April 23, 2020, https://dictionary.apa.org/recency -effect. See also Peter Russell, *The Brain Book: Know Your Own Mind and How to Use It* (Oxfordshire, UK: Routledge, 2010).

p. 72   *"Great is the art of beginning"*: Henry Wadsworth Longfellow, "Elegiac Verse," from *In the Harbor* (New York: Houghton Mifflin, 1882); available at https://www.hwlongfellow.org/poems _poem.php?pid=310.

p. 72   *"The biggest laugh has to be at the end"*: Jonah Weiner, "Jerry Seinfeld Intends to Die Standing Up," *New York Times Magazine* (video), December 20, 2012.

Chapter 5: All Business Is Show Business

p. 79   *"The medium is the message"*: Marshall McLuhan introduced this iconic phrase in his book *Understanding Media: The Extensions of Man* (1964; repr., MIT Press, 1994), 8.

p. 79   *"The room is doing 80 percent of the job"*: Jerry Seinfeld, "Jerry Seinfeld, NBA," *ESPN Radio* (podcast), http://www.espn.com /espnradio/play/_/id/13010973.

p. 84   *Master of Mind Mapping*: Brian Weller, personal communication with the author, April 20, 2020.

p. 89   *what psychologists call the "reminiscence effect"*: Peter Russell, *The Brain Book: Know Your Own Mind and How to Use It* (Oxfordshire, UK: Routledge, 1986), 85–86.

Chapter 6: Words Matter

p. 95   *"I am about to — or I am going to — die"*: "Last Words of Real People," Bailly to Burbank section, website, http://www.sanft leben.com/Last%20Words/lastwords-r-b.html.

p. 97   *"The first man who compared a woman to a rose"*: Though widely attributed to Gérard de Nerval, this quote has also been attributed to Voltaire and Salvador Dalí.

p. 97   *"All writing is a campaign"*: Martin Amis, "Battling Banality," *The Guardian*, March 24, 2001, https://www.theguardian.com /books/2001/mar/24/artsandhumanities.highereducation.

p. 98   *"I don't know and I don't care"*: William Safire, *On Language* (New York: Times Books, 1980), 151.

p. 98   *"So what? Why should I care about what you're saying?"*: Tammy Gales, personal communication with the author, February 14, 2020.

p. 102   *"What we need now is some new, fresh clichés"*: Samuel Goldwyn, as quoted in George Tiffin, *All the Best Lines: An Informal History of the Movies in Quotes, Notes, and Anecdotes* (London: Head of Zeus, 2014). See also "At the End of the Day, Clichés Can Be as Good as Gold," *Talk of the Nation*, NPR, podcast audio, December 27, 2012, https://www.npr.org/2012/12/27/168149099/at-the -end-of-the-day-cliches-can-be-as-good-as-gold.

p. 104   *"If you do it thoughtfully"*: Tammy Gales, personal communication with the author, February 14, 2020.

p. 105   *"There is no mode of action, no form of emotion"*: Oscar Wilde, "The Critic as Artist," in *Oscar Wilde: The Major Works* (New York: Oxford University Press, 2008), 256.

p. 106   *"We can shape events in each other's brains"*: Steven Pinker, *The Language Instinct: How the Mind Creates Language* (William Morrow, 1994; repr., New York: Harper Perennial, 2001), 1.

p. 106   *"A man with a scant vocabulary"*: Henry Hazlitt, *The Wisdom of Henry Hazlitt*, ed. Hans F. Sennholz (Irvington-on-Hudson, NY: The Foundation for Economic Education, 1993), 51.

p. 108   *"In 523 words"*: Greg Hall, "Elizabeth II's Finest Hour," *The Article*, April 6, 2020, https://www.thearticle.com/elizabeth -iis-finest-hour.

p. 109   *"The most important thing is to read"*: J. K. Rowling, online interview, *Scholastic*, February 3, 2000, https://www.scholastic.com /teachers/articles/teaching-content/jk-rowling-interview.

p. 109   *"A good vocabulary is not acquired by reading books"*: *The Letters of J. R. R. Tolkien*, ed. Humphrey Carpenter, (Boston: Mariner Books, 2000), xvi.

Chapter 7: Cultivate Your Body Language

p. 114   *"Humans and other animals express power"*: Dana R. Carney, Amy J. C. Cuddy, and Andy J. Yap, "Power Posing: Brief Nonverbal Displays Affect Neuroendocrine Levels and Risk Tolerance," *Psychological Science* 21, no. 10 (2010): 1363–68, https://www.ncbi .nlm.nih.gov/pubmed/20855902. Watch Cuddy's TED Talk, which has received more than 57 million views, here: https:// www.ted.com/talks/amy_cuddy_your_body_language_may _shape_who_you_are. This talk sparked significant criticism. You can read her response at David Biello, "Inside the Debate about Power Posing: A Q & A with Amy Cuddy," Ideas.TED .com, February 22, 2017, https://ideas.ted.com/inside-the-debate -about-power-posing-a-q-a-with-amy-cuddy.

p. 116   *In a study entitled "Attracting Assault"*: Betty Grayson and Morris I. Stein, "Attracting Assault: Victims' Nonverbal Cues," *Journal of Communication* 31, no. 1 (1981): 68–75, https://academic.oup.com /joc/article-abstract/31/1/68/4371921?redirectedFrom=fulltext. See also Carol Krucoff, "YOU: Sending Out Messages of Muggability?," *The Washington Post*, December 9, 1980, https://www .washingtonpost.com/archive/lifestyle/1980/12/09/you-sending -out-messages-of-muggability/c4ad2149-474e-446a-bf3b-3d90f b18b89e.

p. 128   *"We join spokes together in a wheel"*: Lao Tzu, *Tao Te Ching: A New English Version*, trans. Stephen Mitchell (New York: Harper & Row, 1998), 11.

p. 129   *"That impressive silence, that eloquent silence"*: Mark Twain, *Autobiography of Mark Twain*, vol. 3 (Oakland, CA: University of California Press, 2015), 170.

p. 130   *"a means for changing stereotyped response patterns"*: Frank Jones, "Method for Changing Stereotyped Response Patterns by the Inhibition of Certain Postural Sets," *Psychological Review* 72, no. 3 (May 1965): 196–214.

p. 130   *"a method for expanding consciousness"*: Frank Pierce Jones, *Body Awareness in Action: A Study of the Alexander Technique* (New York: Schocken, 1976), 2.

p. 131   *"the method for keeping your eye on the ball applied to life"*: Leo Stein in Jones, *Body Awareness in Action*, 48.

p. 134   *"My daily practice of the Balanced Resting State"*: Deborah Domanski, personal communication with the author, April 11, 2020. Note: Domanski is my wife. I listen to her exquisite singing every day. I also get to hear the improvement in her students' voices.

p. 136   *laughter is one of the best ways*: "Social Laughter Releases Endorphins in the Brain," *ScienceDaily*, June 1, 2007, https://www.sciencedaily.com/releases/2017/06/170601124121.htm.

p. 137   *listening to the music you lLove*: Laura Ferreri et al., "Dopamine Modulates the Reward Experiences Elicited by Music," *PNAS* 116, no. 9 (2019): 3793–98, https://www.pnas.org/content/116/9/3793.

p. 137   *The scents of lavender and vanilla*: "10 Natural Ways to Release Endorphins Instantly," *Reader's Digest*, https://www.rd.com/health/wellness/natural-endorphin-boosters.

p. 137   *Anticipating celebration raises dopamine levels*: Thai Nguyen, "Hacking into Your Happy Chemicals: Dopamine, Serotonin, Endorphins and Oxytocin," *HuffPost*, October 20, 2014, updated December 6, 2017, https://www.huffpost.com/entry/hacking-into-your-happy-c_b_6007660.

p. 138   *"These simple practices can help you gain control"*: Eva Selhub, personal communication with the author, March 13, 2020.

p. 138   *Karsenty explains that our bones release the hormone osteocalcin*: Gerard Karsenty et al., "Mediation of the Acute Stress Response by the Skeleton," *Cell Metabolism* 30, no. 5 (2019), https://www.cell.com/cell-metabolism/fulltext/S1550-4131(19)30441-3.

Chapter 8: If the Buddha Gave Sales Presentations

p. 142   *"Sales scams are as old as humanity"*: Better Business Bureau, "Sales Scams," https://www.bbb.org/pacific-southwest/get-consumer -help/top-scams/sales-scams.

p. 143   *"I was lucky enough to find someone who believed in me"*: Jeff Kriendler, "Frank W. Abagnale: Pan Am's Great Impostor," in *Pan Am: Personal Tributes to a Global Aviation Pioneer*, ed. Jeff Kriendler and James Patrick Baldwin (San Francisco: Pan Am Historical Foundation, 2017), 78; available at https://www .abagnale.com/pdf/KriendlerAbagnale.pdf.

p. 144   *"Be sure…you can answer the two questions"*: Daniel H. Pink, *To Sell Is Human: The Surprising Truth about Moving Others* (New York: Riverhead, 2012), 228.

p. 144   *"Sales must be the ultimate ethical"*: Steve Lishansky, personal communication with the author, March 13, 2020.

p. 146   *"Maybe you don't hold the title of salesperson"*: Zig Ziglar, "Everyone Sells," *Success*, May 12, 2009, https://www.success.com/everyone -sells.

p. 146   *"Physicians sell patients on a remedy"*: Pink, *To Sell Is Human*, 19.

p. 147   *"the use of one person's communication skills"*: Duane Sparks, per- sonal communication with the author, March 13, 2020.

p. 148   *"For years, our most successful partners"*: Chris Hillmann, personal communication with the author, April 2, 2020.

p. 148   *"Most people, even many within the world of formal sales"*: Sparks, personal communication, March 13, 2020.

p. 149   *He's discovered that although most people believe*: Robert B. Cialdini, *Influence: The Psychology of Persuasion* (1984; repr., New York: Harper Business, 2006).

p. 151   *"It is the spread of the good things"*: Nicholas A. Christakis, TED Talk, "The Hidden Influence of Social Networks," May 10, 2010, https://www.youtube.com/watch?v=2U-tOghblfE.

p. 154   *"On the one hand, seeming too eager might be taken"*: Jeremy Nicholson, personal communication with the author, Febru- ary 14, 2020.

p. 157   *"evolutionary adaptation, the need to figure out"*: Nalini Ambady and Robert Rosenthal, "Half a Minute: Predicting Teacher Evaluations from Thin Slices of Nonverbal Behavior and Physical Attractiveness," *Journal of Personality and Social Psychology* 64, no. 3 (1993): 431–41.

p. 158   *"Individuals tend to look at what other people are doing"*: Nicholson, personal communication, February 14, 2020.

p. 160   *"You can do much on behalf of your own healing"*: *A Course in Miracles*, ed. Helen Schucman, Bill Thetford, and Kenneth Wapnick (New York: Foundation for Inner Peace, 1976), 28.

Conclusion: The Master's Secret Mirror

p. 163   *"In the master's secret mirror"*: George Leonard, *Mastery: The Keys to Success and Long-Term Fulfillment* (New York: Plume, 1992), 176.

p. 163   *"I think I'm beginning to understand something about painting"*: "Renoir Art Lesson — Biography and Activities," *Liberty Hill House* (blog), October 9, 2015, http://www.libertyhillhouse.com /2015/10/09/renoir-art-lesson-biography-activities.

p. 168   *"You can learn from an ordinary bamboo leaf"*: Eugen Herrigel, *Zen in the Art of Archery*, trans. R. F. C. Hull (1953; repr., Vigeo Press, 2018), 48.

p. 168   *"must fall from the archer"*: Ibid.

p. 168   *"The best moments in our lives are not the passive"*: Mihály Csíkszentmihályi, *Flow: The Psychology of Optimal Experience* (New York: Harper Perennial, 2008), 3.

Questions and Answers

p. 174   *"Very early on in my career, I hit upon this idea"*: Sean Davis, "Jerry Seinfeld Explains the Perfect Way to Handle Donald Trump," *The Federalist*, September 10, 2015, https://thefederalist .com/2015/09/10/jerry-seinfeld-explains-the-perfect-way-to -handle-donald-trump.

Recommended Resources

Mind Mapping and Creative Thinking

Brian Weller, https://brianjweller.com
Video seminar on thinking like Leonardo da Vinci,
https://geniusmastery.com

Facility with Language

Tammy Gales, forensicling.com
Steven Pinker, *The Sense of Style: The Thinking Person's Guide
to Writing in the 21st Century*

The Alexander Technique

Workshops around the world: https://alexandertechnique
workshops.com
Michael J. Gelb, *Body Learning: An Introduction to the Alexander
Technique*, 2nd ed.; available at https://michaelgelb
.com/resources

Voice Coaching

Beret Arcaya, http://www.habitandchoice.com/about.html
Deborah Domanski, https://www.deborahdomanski.com

Stress Management, Resilience, and Presence

Lorie Dechar, https://www.anewpossibility.com
Patty de Llosa, https://pattydellosa.com
Eva Selhub, https://www.drselhub.com
Shauna Shapiro, https://drshaunashapiro.com

Sales and Influence

Robert B. Cialdini, *Influence: The Psychology of Persuasion*,
    https://www.influenceatwork.com
Steve Lishansky, *The Ultimate Sales Revolution: Sell Differently.*
    Change the World, https://www.optimizeintl.com
Harvey Mackay, https://harveymackay.com
Jeremy Nicholson, https://www.psychologytoday.com/us
    /experts/jeremy-nicholson-msw-phd
Daniel H. Pink, *To Sell Is Human: The Surprising Truth about*
    Moving Others, https://www.danpink.com
Duane Sparks, https://www.actionselling.com

Public Speaking Groups

Toastmasters, https://www.toastmasters.org
National Speakers Association, https://www.nsaspeaker.org

Index

Page references given in *italics* indicate illustrations.

Washington Redskins (football
    team), 24–25
Watts, Alan, 108
Weaver, Sigourney, 131
weight distribution, 119
Weller, Brian, xiii, 84
"whatever," 102, 103
"When all is said and done," 100
"When push comes to shove,"
    99–100
whiteboards, 80
Wilde, Oscar, 105, 109
"With all due respect," 102
Wodehouse, P. G., 109
"woke," 101
Woodward, Joanne, 131

word origins, 106–7
World Memory Championships, 43
writing, 30, 42
writing skills, 1, 2, 20

Yeats, William Butler, 30
Yelp, 142
Young Presidents' Organization
    (YPO), 107
Yousafzai, Malala, 10

Zak, Paul J., 69
Zen in the Art of Archery (Herrigel),
    168
Zeus (Greek deity), 43
Ziglar, Zig, 146

About the Author

Michael J. Gelb is a professional public speaker renowned for his scintillating, inspiring, and life-changing presentations on creative leadership, genius thinking, and conscious business. He has served as an executive leadership and presentation coach to AT&T, DuPont, Genentech, KPMG, Merck, Microsoft, Nike, YPO, and many others.

Michael is the author of seventeen books, including *How to Think Like Leonardo da Vinci*, *The Art of Connection*, *Body Learning*, and *The Healing Organization*, coauthored with Raj Sisodia. Michael's books have been translated into twenty-five languages and have sold more than a million copies.

In 2003 Michael received a Batten Fellowship in Innovation from the University of Virginia, and he codirected the acclaimed Leading Innovation Seminar at the Darden Graduate School of Business for more than ten years. In April 2020 he accepted the role of Senior Fellow at the Center for Humanistic Management and became a member of the Leading People and Organizations Advisory Board at the Fordham University Gabelli School of

Business. He teaches for the Gabelli School and for the London Business School.

Michael is a master teacher of the Alexander Technique, a fifth-degree black belt in aikido, and a gifted teacher of qigong and tai chi. He is also a professional juggler who has performed with the Rolling Stones.

www.michaelgelb.com
www.healingleader.com